C.E.S. Dandridge.

1st February, 1985.

Creative Papercraft

Creative
Papercraft

Stuart E. Grainger

BLANDFORD PRESS
Poole   **Dorset**

First published in the U.K. 1980

Copyright © 1980 Blandford Press Ltd.
Link House, West Street,
Poole, Dorset, BH15 1LL

ISBN 0 7137 1008 X

(Typeset 11 on 12pt Monotype Bell and printed and
bound in England by Staples Printers Rochester
Limited at The Stanhope Press)

Contents

Foreword

'Please will you make us a camel's head? . . . and she must look glamorous.' That request from my small daughter, preparing for a Brownie Guide concert, was the first of a long succession of similarly bizarre demands over several years. The first line of defence protecting her innocently flattering confidence that 'Daddy could do it' was my interest in and knowledge, perforce acquired, of paper sculpture techniques. The relatively low cost of paper or card and the speed with which a satisfactory product could be achieved soon proved that, as a medium for constructing 'props' for plays, fêtes, and carnivals, paper has no equal.

Some years later, when asked by The Handcrafts Advisory Association for the Disabled to provide instruction in paper sculpture, I included among the projects, in addition to the more esoteric artistic designs, plans for a number of the practical items which had been evolved. The practical ideas have proved to be, if anything, the more popular with the instructors of the disabled, who are my students. These designs have been carefully documented, therefore, and some have been developed still further, leading to yet more. Many small mistakes in the original drawings have been eliminated because they were discovered 'the hard way' by an enthusiastic student who drew the error to my attention, usually with unjustified politeness.

Eventually finding myself photocopying some fifty pages of drawings for every student, it seemed that publication would be genuinely in response to demand, but the practical designs would have been of little value without also supplying the preliminary means of developing the skills and understanding the techniques of basic paper sculpture. Chapters 1 to 4 of this book set out to provide information about tools, materials and techniques, together with a series of progressively more ambitious projects, from simple pictorial relief to quite complicated free-standing figures.

Chapters 5 to 10 provide a series of designs demonstrating the more practical applications of the techniques developed in the first part of the book. The designs in Chapters 5 to 10 are not arranged with any consideration of their relative ease or difficulty in construction, but in categories of usage — picture frames, stage 'props', toys and so on — for where the first part dealt with paper and the way to handle it, the second part establishes the purpose to which the skills acquired can be put.

It must be made clear that this is not intended as a comprehensive catalogue of either techniques or applications. New and original ways of using paper are still to be discovered and there may be old ways which have been overlooked or deliberately omitted — papier mâché, for instance. Similarly the purposes described are but a few of the innumerable possibilities which exist. Creative minds will be able to enlarge the repertoire far beyond what is suggested here, and that is the real purpose of this book. Whether acknowledged as art or craft, sculpture or mere construction, the activity of using paper as a creative medium will continue only so long as there is interest in it; stimulating that interest is the function of the pages which follow.

1 Basic Materials and Tools

Paper

In its pure and basic form, paper sculpture uses only paper and glue as raw materials and a very limited number of simple tools with which to work. The fundamental raw material in this context is good quality cartridge paper, of a weight and texture suitable for the particular project in hand. For practising and developing ideas and for many small-scale designs, ordinary cartridge paper of 110 grammes per square metre (the equivalent in the old descriptive system of about 70 lb paper) is easily obtainable in rolls from stationers, artists' and drawing office suppliers and printers. It costs rather more in pads or sheets, but may be more convenient in these forms for many people, being easier to handle and store. For larger work, particularly free-standing, self-supporting pieces, heavier, more expensive material will be needed. Cartridge paper of 150 gsm and 200 gsm, is readily obtainable from drawing office suppliers, in rolls 841 mm (33 in.) wide by 25 m (82 ft) long, as well as in pads and sheets.

Two better quality papers, which can be recommended and are widely available from artists' suppliers in single sheets measuring 560 × 760 mm (29¾ × 22 in.), are known by their brand names of 'Fabriano', which is made in Italy, and 'Bockingford', which is made in Britain. Both of these papers have very pleasing surface textures, 'Bockingford' being rougher and softer, where 'Fabriano' is crisper, with the added advantages of a range of colours and a slightly cheaper price at the time of writing, although neither of these excellent materials can be regarded as cheap by any standard. Both are delightful to work with and produce a good looking finished article. Remember, though, that there is little point in buying an expensive paper if you intend to paint the finished product, as the most attractive feature of good paper is its surface texture.

A cheaper alternative with equivalent strength, but having a less attractive texture and not so pleasant to work, is provided by ordinary white or tinted three or four sheet card, which is almost universally obtainable from retailers and printers, and is quite good enough for most practical, as opposed to purely artistic, purposes.

Tinted Ingres papers are attractive in appearance, but are rather hard and brittle to work with, although available in a wide variety of shades and weights. Ingres papers may be satisfactory for simple shapes and are excellent for backgrounds, in which situation a very much cheaper alternative may be found in what are known as 'sugar' papers. Sugar papers have little 'body', are difficult to work satisfactorily, and damage easily, so they are not really suitable for anything but background use.

If no expense is to be spared, there are hand-made papers available from specialist artists' suppliers, which will do justice to the finest work — and to which only the finest work may do justice — but, taking a more 'cheap and cheerful' approach, bargains are often to be found in decorators' and D.I.Y. suppliers, among the odd rolls of left-over wallpapers.

To the paper sculpture purist, that is about as far as choice is permissible. However, even the purist must admit that heavy card, 'ticket' board and mounting boards, which are obtainable from artists' suppliers and printers in a wide range of colours, are necessary for backgrounds and bases, particularly in pictorial relief work.

Those of us who are of a more practical turn of mind feel no shame in using any material that suits our purpose and that does not detract from the appearance of the finished product. A later chapter deals with many 'allied' materials in detail, but, as we are considering 'basic' materials here, it is reasonable to mention ordinary brown cardboard and corrugated paper such as are commonly used for packaging. These humble materials are of great value for the inexpensive formation of a hidden framework, upon which a superstructure of artistically acceptable appearance may be supported. The sculptor in clay normally uses a matrix of wire and, similarly, the sculptor in paper may use cardboard or, indeed, any other suitable substance to provide the internal strength his work may require.

Glue

There is such a wide range of glues available, under numerous brand names, that it would be wrong to be too categorical. However, as it is essential to provide clear guidance here, colourless quick-drying glues, such as 'Bostik No. 1' or 'Uhu', are recommended for most purposes. Latex adhesives such as 'Copydex' are also generally satisfactory and have the advantage of being easily removed without making a mess, if they have been too generously applied; however, they dry more slowly and, being flexible, do not provide much structural rigidity. P.V.A. adhesives can also be used and are quite suitable for glueing large areas, but again dry too slowly for many purposes. Some papers absorb slow-drying or liquid glues and are liable to distort, swell or become limp as a result. For great strength and structural rigidity, the '2 pot' quick-setting epoxy resin adhesives, such as Araldite 'Rapid' and Devcon '5 Minute', are excellent, but they are expensive and not suitable for general use.

Although most glues are cheaper when bought in bulk, it may not be good economic policy always to buy in large containers. Often a medium-sized tube is the best buy, as it provides a greater degree of control, thus avoiding waste and problems in removing inadvertent drips from work, clothing, surroundings and self. Whatever the glue, the one working rule invariably to be followed is — 'Read the instructions first.' Many glues are highly inflammable, many are irritants to sensitive skin, some are almost impossible to remove when set and others are liable to dissolve when paint is applied. Let the voice of experience warn you that an intricate piece of sculpture can be reduced by the over-enthusiastic application of aerosol paint into a disaster of sticky, but unstuck, pieces of paper!

Tools and Working Aids

Scissors are the first essential, and the most useful all-purpose type for cutting paper, as for many other crafts, is that which is sold specifically for barbers and hairdressers. The blades are straight, relatively long and narrow, pointed enough for delicate work, yet not so pointed as to be easily capable of doing accidental damage. A smaller pair of sharp pointed scissors, perhaps a pair of curved nail-scissors, and even a pair of pinking shears will be found useful occasionally, but with all cutting tools it is a good rule to buy the best that you can afford, look after them with care and keep them sharp.

The last three words are of even greater importance when applied to your knife or knives, so craft knives with blades that can be easily replaced are recommended, as these can (and should) be kept razor sharp. In Britain, at least three suitable designs of 'Stanley' craft knife handles are widely available, which can be fitted with blades of various shapes. Stanley knife blades, pattern numbers 5901, 5903 or 5905 are probably best for fine work, ideally fitted into a handle which allows the blade to be retracted or folded away when not in use, both for safety and to protect the blade. Other brand names of suitable knives

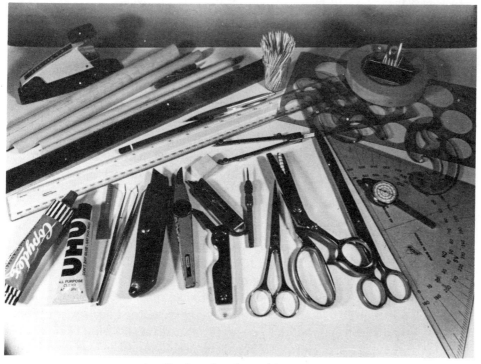

A collection of tools used in papercraft.

11

available in Britain are 'Swann Morton', 'Uni-Tool' and 'X-acto', but there are certainly several others which are equally satisfactory, the important criteria for choice being a really sharp cutting edge, a sharp point, a comfortable handle and a means of protecting the blade when not in use.

For cutting heavier materials it can be convenient to have a second knife with a larger and stronger blade and, again, there are many types to choose from. A cobbler's knife, or the type with a curved pointed blade sold by many hardware shops for cutting linoleum would be suitable.

A steel straight-edge, preferably 50 cm (or 18 in.) long, is highly recommended for use as a guide for your knife when cutting or scoring along straight lines. An ordinary wooden or plastic graduated measuring rule is essential, not only for measuring and drawing straight lines, but also to use as a tool for curling.

For curling or curving across a fair width of paper, a rolling technique is recommended, and for this a base of fairly soft, but resilient, and clean material, such as felt, sponge rubber, carpet or underlay is required. The dimensions of this are not very important, but a rectangle, say 30 cm (12 in.) square and about 1 to 2 cm ($\frac{1}{2}$–$\frac{3}{4}$ in.) thick would be suitable. The actual rolling tools are lengths of wood dowelling, about 30 to 40 cm (12–16 in.) long, of diameters varying from, say, 6 mm ($\frac{1}{4}$ in.) up to 25 mm (1 in.). To start with, a single roller of 12 or 15 mm (about $\frac{1}{2}$ in.) in diameter will do very well, but you will find with experience that you will probably collect other useful sizes.

It is most important to have a good flat, clear and clean working surface and also a piece of material upon which you can cut with a sharp knife and a clear conscience, knowing that you will not damage the furniture. A pad of newspaper or old magazines, a rectangle of hardboard, strawboard or chipboard are all equally suitable, as they are inexpensive and can be easily replaced, as indeed they should be when the surface starts to break up. Cork, blockboard, insulation board and plywood will also provide satisfactory, but more expensive, cutting surfaces. Some authorities recommend glass, but, apart from being easily cracked by a casually dropped tool, glass is a slippery and very hard surface upon which a point or edge can easily slip accidentally (and dangerously) and will quickly become dull.

Drawing Instruments

In the design stages a few straightforward drawing instruments are necessary. A graduated rule has already been mentioned and pencils are obvious items. Remember, however, that everything must be kept as clean as possible, and any pencil marks on the outside of the finished product must be removed, so use a soft pencil — B or 2B — and do not press heavily. A good quality soft rubber eraser is essential. Strong, but not necessarily expensive, drawing compasses, a large 45° set square and a protractor will be useful. Another useful, although not essential, designing instrument is a map measuring wheel; this is a small wheel geared to a needle which moves over a graduated dial, enabling one to measure the length of curved lines accurately. A template with which small circles can be drawn easily is a very useful asset and some people find a set of French curves helpful. A final essential item is tracing paper, or a reasonable equivalent. It is not often required in very large pieces, so that a pad of A5 size will satisfy most needs, but tracing paper is an invaluable aid in developing a design and checking that one piece will fit accurately alongside another.

Other Working Aids

Every artist and craftsman uses a few unconventional tools or working aids which particularly suit him, but which may not be of value to others working in the same medium. The items I have already mentioned are, in the main, essentials or in common use, but there are several other potentially useful items, many quite obvious, some less so. It would be impossible to list every item which may come in useful, but such a list would almost certainly include the following:

A fairly large-gauge knitting needle, perhaps broken to about the length of a pencil, or a piece of dowelling, about 6 mm ($\frac{1}{4}$ in.) in diameter and sharpened at one end.

A wooden or plastic paper knife, plastic palette knife, or flat bladed clay modelling tool.

Paper clips, of all types.

Glass headed pins.

Elastic bands.

Galvanised or plastic coated flexible wire.

A lump of 'Plasticine'.

A box of wooden or plastic cocktail sticks.

A roll of masking tape.

An 'office type' staple gun.

Tweezers and pliers.

Sprung clothes pegs.

2 Shaping Techniques

The use of paper, a strictly two-dimensional material, to form three-dimensional objects, requires a certain understanding of the limitations imposed by the medium. These limitations include structural weakness, plain texture and only mono-directional flexibility, all of which can be overcome by a few simple techniques. It must be understood also that the shape of a volume can be delineated or made apparent only in terms of what the eye can see or the fingers discern, which is only the surface and outline of the real volume. It is that surface and outline which our paper must simultaneously both provide and support, for we set ourselves the task of making bodies from skin alone, or, at best, of skin with a very few bones beneath, the flesh being non-existent and mere illusion. It is in this illusion that the real skill of paper sculpture lies.

There are five basic techniques used in working with paper — cutting, folding, rolling, overlapping, and distorting.

Cutting

Cutting is, of course, the means by which the area of a piece of paper is physically defined and, for our purposes, it is normally done by means of a knife or a pair of scissors. Whilst scissors are often more convenient to use, a sharp knife will usually produce a cleaner line and is more accurate, particularly for delicate work. It is advisable for the beginner to pencil the intended cutting line on the paper before cutting, and then to remove the pencil marks with a clean eraser if they are visible on the outside of the work. Straight lines are best cut with a knife along a steel straight-edge.

Where complicated outlines are to be cut, start by cutting around the whole piece with scissors and then cut the detail with a knife. Whenever using a knife always cut on a piece of board or a pad of paper which does not matter, and keep the fingers of the hand which is not holding the knife behind the cutting edge and never in front of it. It can not be over-emphasised that all cutting tools should be kept as sharp as possible.

Scoring and Folding

Scoring is, strictly speaking, a cutting technique, but it is only of use when paper is to be folded, and its purpose is to ensure a clean, crisp fold that does not waver or wrinkle. Scoring is done by running a knife edge lightly along a line on the paper, in such a way that only part of the thickness of the material is cut. When the paper is then folded away from the scored line, the cut edges open, and the material folds easily and cleanly along the weakened line. Scoring should always be done on the outside of the fold, as it is far less effective on the inside. Always

15

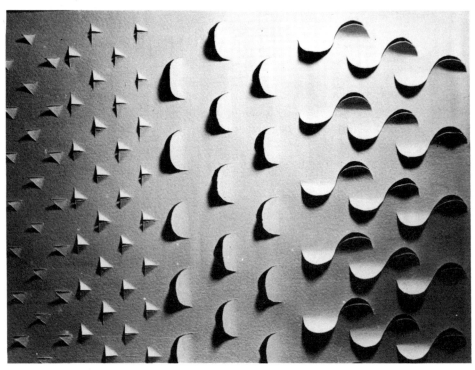

Surface textures. The effects produced by a series of simple cuts, pressed upwards from underneath.

precede folding by scoring, as it is very difficult to produce a neat fold without scoring it first, and crisp, well-executed folds are essential in producing a good paper sculpture.

Folding may have a variety of purposes and it also has a variety of effects. It always alters the plane of the paper's surface and, in doing so, produces a line of rigidity along a plane between the two surface planes, providing greatly increased structural strength in resisting flexing and compression along the line of the fold. Folded tabs are often the means by which one piece is connected to another, either by inserting tabs on one piece into slots in the surface of an adjoining piece, or by glueing the tabs beneath the adjoining surface. Interlocking folds may be used also to join two pieces together without glueing. Alternating the direction of folds is a means of providing great elasticity, as in the bellows of accordions and concertinas, and at the same time enormously increasing the surface strength of the structure. Similarly, a sheet of paper alternately 'concertina' folded and then formed into a tube, produces a pillar of a strength out of all proportion to the flimsy material from which it is made. Such 'concertina' folding is one way of producing a more interesting surface texture, and, if cutting and folding are combined, an almost infinite variety of surface textures can be produced.

Rolling and Curling

A sheet of paper rolled into a tube in the hand and then released will spring back into its original flat form. If it is to remain in a tubular form, the structure of the paper itself has to be distorted, and there are two basic ways in which this may be done.

The easiest and most reliable way is to place the sheet of paper on a pad of some resilient material, such as carpeting or foam rubber, lay on top of it a length of rod or tube, dowelling or broom handle, and roll this with a slight pressure to and fro over the paper, as though rolling out pastry. The paper tends to distort in conformity with the curve of the roller, and the smaller the diameter of the roller, the tighter the paper will curl. This method offers no problems and is the best means of inducing a curve in a large area of paper.

A second method of curling is to pull the paper over a blunt edge, such as that of a wooden ruler or the back of the blade of a pair of scissors, or even the edge of a table or desk. This works well with a strip or a corner, when it is fairly easy to maintain an even tension over the blunt edge, but over a large area it is difficult with this method to avoid unevenness and ribbing. The technique is to lay the paper down on a firm, flat surface, and, taking hold of one edge, draw it smoothly upwards against the edge of the wooden or plastic ruler, which is held with slight pressure angled against the flat surface. The difficulty of this manoeuvre lies in holding the ruler steady at the right angle and pressure with one hand, while the other hand withdraws the paper smoothly and steadily in a flowing movement. Any hesitant or erratic movement causes an uneven curve to develop and the possibility of creases in the paper. A fairly narrow strip, up to about 3 cm (1 in.) wide, or a corner, can be curled by drawing it between the thumb and the back of a scissors blade or ruler edge. The action must be smooth and decisive, for any hesitation will produce a line or rib in the curve.

The purpose of rolling or curling may be purely visual or decorative, but it may be used, in conjunction with overlapping and glueing, to produce a tube, scroll or spiral, or combinations of these. A curve in the paper surface has similar, although in degree much smaller, effects upon the structural strength as has a fold. A tubular section has considerable strength to resist flexing and compression along its length.

Overlapping and Glueing

Overlapping is the normal method of joining edges and ends together in paper sculpture, the overlap usually being secured by glue. Overlaps may also be secured without glue, by interlocking folds, interlocking slots or tabs and slots, when a fastening capable of being disengaged and re-connected is required, for instance on boxes, masks, garlands and similar items of a more practical nature.

A series of glued overlaps can be particularly useful in providing a means of curving a structure in two dimensions; indeed it is sometimes the only satisfactory way of producing such a contour. A good illustration of this principle is

Curling with roller and pad.

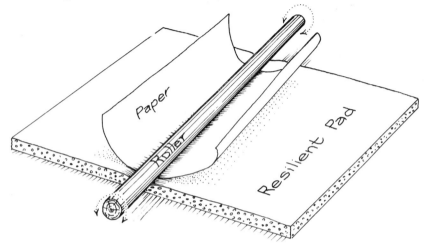

Curling in the hand.

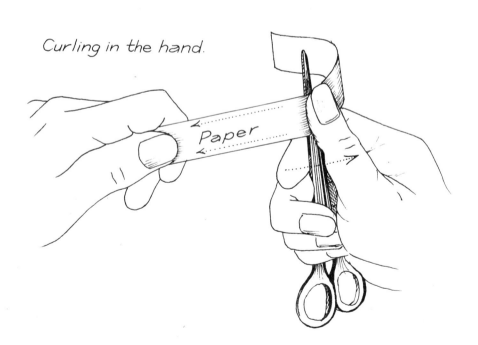

available in an old-fashioned 'clinker built' rowing boat, where flat planks, curving between bow and stern, were fastened together overlapping along their edges to provide a curve from keel to gunwale. The same principle may be observed in a bird's wing, where the feathers overlap and provide flexible curves between wingtip and body, from the leading edge to the trailing edge.

Overlapping strips or folds may also be used effectively to provide surface texture and increased strength. The advantages and disadvantages of various types of glue have been discussed in Chapter 1. However, the way in which a glue is used is also of vital importance in producing a satisfactory article. Always read and follow the maker's instructions, and use only as much glue as you really need. Spilled and wasted glue is the most common fault to be found on paper sculpture and it is usually better to use too little glue rather than too much.

Distorting, Denting, Bruising and Stretching

These distorting techniques are not often encountered, mainly because few papers allow them to be used to much purpose. Soft thick papers, such as heavy Bockingford, some wallpapers and blotting papers, do allow themselves to be shaped to some extent by hammering with a ball pane hammer, furrowing with a blunt pointed wooden or plastic tool and even some embossing or repoussé work using special tools, in much the same way as one can work soft metallic foils. It is not easy to give firm guidance on these techniques, as so much depends upon the material. The best rule is, if in doubt, experiment with a small piece first.

The purpose of these techniques is mainly to provide interesting surface textures. It is possible, however, to produce shallow domes or a concave shape by bruising and stretching, and a frilled effect can be produced by stretching the edge. Stretching a paper can often be achieved more easily when it is wet, and limited areas can be dampened with a small sponge. Care must be taken, however, when working on damp paper, as it is all too easy to tear it in this condition. Remember too that it will tend to shrink again as it dries.

Embossing addresses on writing paper has, of course, long been used in commerce and embossed paper seals are also commonplace, but this requires very accurately positioned and produced metal dies which must be used in specially engineered presses. It is not too difficult, however, to produce perfectly satisfactory dies by carving a design in hardwood and moulding the matching relief die in plaster or glass reinforced resin, but whether the resulting embossed paper can be regarded as paper sculpture must be doubtful.

Only one kind of paper is made with the specific property of allowing permanent distortion by stretching, and that is, of course, crêpe paper. Again, whether crêpe paper can be regarded as a suitable medium for paper sculpture is a matter of personal opinion, but there are certainly large areas within the definition of papercraft which would be barren without the existence of crêpe paper, and when used in conjunction with true paper sculpture, crêpe paper techniques are invaluable for many practical purposes.

19

3 Design and Construction

Whatever the shape of the completed sculpture may be, it must have sufficient inbuilt strength to support itself. One very straightforward way in which to provide strength for paper sculpture is to work a picture in relief using a background board to supply all the support needed for the sculpted design, which is glued to the background and protrudes outward from it towards the viewer.

Almost any subject may be treated in this way and it is certainly the best first step for the beginner, allowing a freedom of design, without regard to strength, that helps one to become familiar with the peculiarities of paper. Leaves, fishes, masks and heraldic devices are among the many effective designs which readily lend themselves to this treatment. Scrolls and medallions, either by themselves or intermixed with other features, can be used to decorate a variety of articles, such as presentation boxes and handsome frames for pictures and photographs. Some examples are provided here for practice, but try designing your own as well, because that is by far the best way to find out what can and cannot be done with paper.

Leaves, being naturally almost two-dimensional, can be imitated very closely with paper, but even so simple a subject requires care when scoring and folding the creases. Some leaves only need to be scored on one side, and here you should note that the obverse side showing in the diagram or plan may be, as often as not, the back or reverse of the completed piece, thus ensuring that as few pencil marks as possible appear on the front of the work. When scoring on both sides is indicated, complete all the scoring before you start any folding. On leaves it is best to fold the central vein first, followed by the other score lines on the back of the leaf, before those on the front, because the lines on the back are the most prominent veins of a leaf, its skeleton in fact.

Where pecked and dotted lines indicate that scoring on the reverse side is necessary, the course of these lines often can be transferred most conveniently to the reverse side by pressing the point of a needle or of a pair of compasses through from the obverse side. Straight lines will need only two such points, one at each end, but curves may require several at intervals along the line. If the scoring on the reverse side is too complicated to be transferred easily by this method, trace the necessary line with a soft pencil on tracing paper and mark three widely separated reference points through both the original and the tracing with a needle point. The tracing then may be turned over and laid on the reverse side of the original, positioned accurately by means of the reference points, and transferred by drawing again over the traced lines visible through the tracing paper.

If the background board of a relief picture is to be painted or covered, this

21

should be done and allowed to dry before attempting to glue the relief figures to it. Sometimes it may be necessary to place one or two folded tabs on the back of the relief figure, where they will not be seen, in order to facilitate glueing, but usually there will be enough points of contact between a relief figure and its background, where glue can be placed, to provide adequate adhesion. Finally, whether the picture is to hang on a wall or stand upright on a table, it will have to be provided with suitable hanging points or supports, which must be strong enough to do the job.

When using the diagrams and plans in this book, please remember the following :-

Lines drawn thus	Indicate
Defined as in the text	
Continuous	Cut along this line. N.B. Expansion grid lines also continuous but drawn thinner.
Pecked	Score along this line on the obverse side and fold or crease.
Pecked & dotted	Score along this line on the reverse side and fold or crease.
o'lap Dotted	Construction advice or measurement.
Interrupted	Centre line, each side "mirrors" the other matching side, although only one may be drawn.

Always fold or crease away from the scored side.

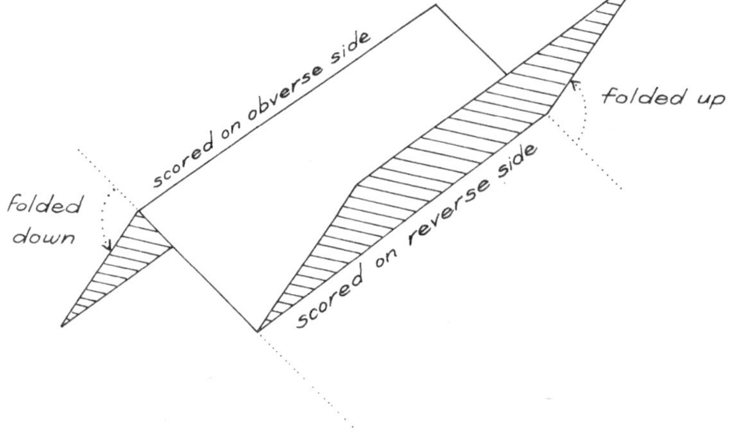

folded down

scored on obverse side

folded up

scored on reverse side

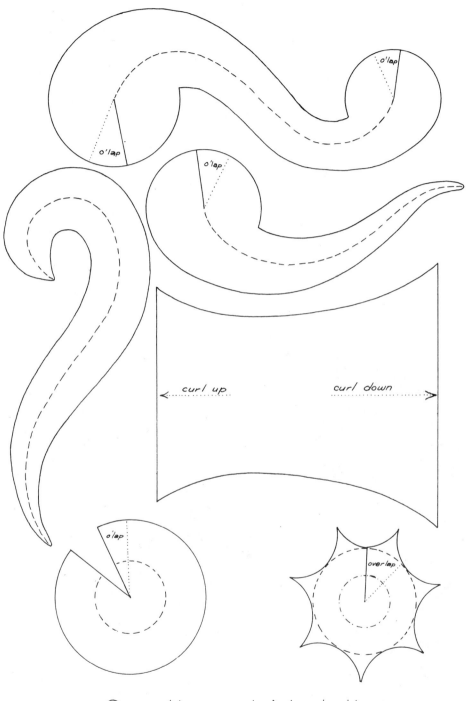

o'lap

o'lap

o'lap

o'lap

curl up ←........................→ *curl down*

o'lap

overlap

Scrolls and Medallions.

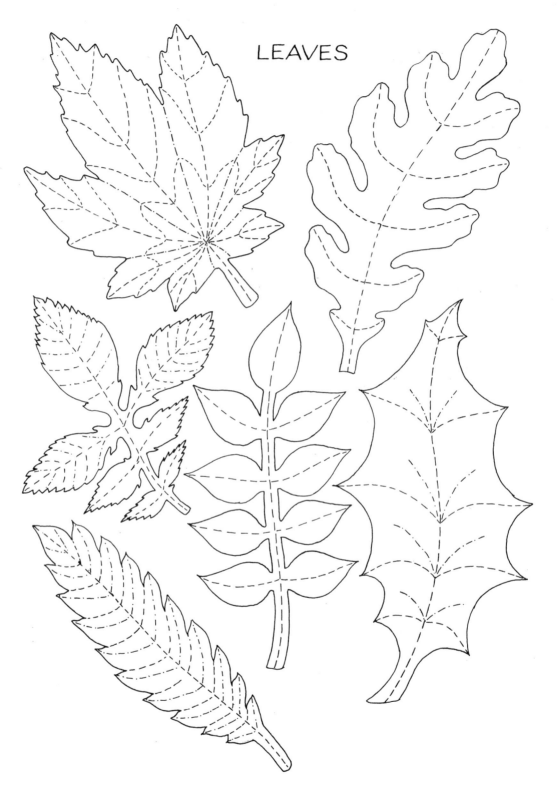

LEAVES

Leaves and a Fir Cone, made in 200 gsm cartridge paper.

An Aquarium. Figures in relief, made in 'Fabriano' paper and mounted on board.

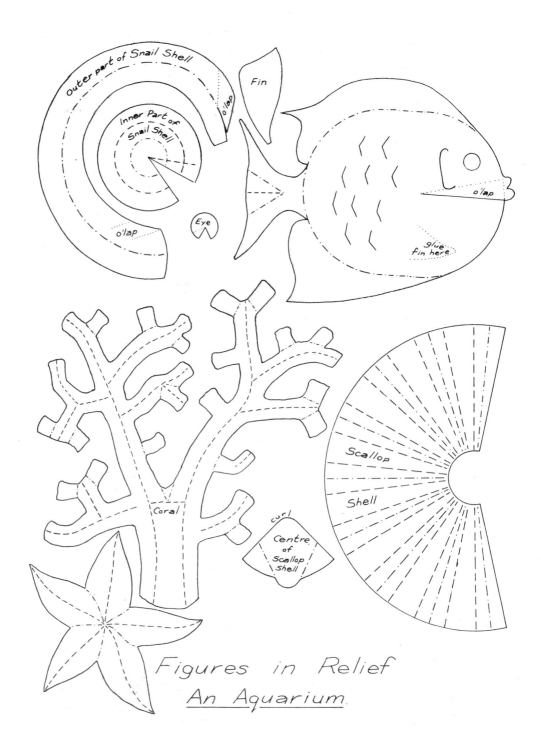

outer part of Snail Shell

o'lap

Fin

Inner Part of
Snail Shell

o'lap

o'lap

Eye

glue
fin here

Scallop

Shell

Coral

curl

Centre
of
Scallop
Shell

Figures in Relief
An Aquarium

Fin

Weed
curl and twist

Tail

Seahorse's
Eye

o'lap

glue
eye
here

overlap

Fish's Eye

glue
under

tail

glue
fin
here

27

The Stag and Tudor Rose. Heraldic devices in relief, made in 'Fabriano' paper and mounted on board.

The Panther Rampant. A heraldic device in relief, made in 'Fabriano' paper and mounted on board.

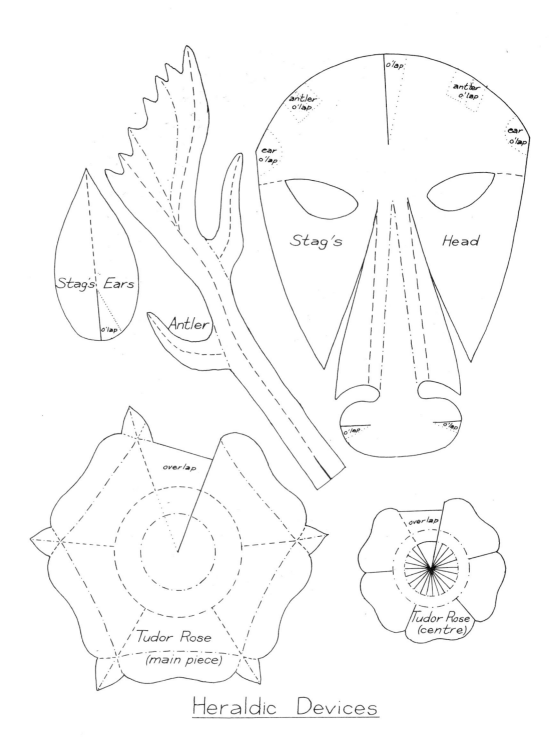

o'lap

antler
o'lap

antler
o'lap

ear
o'lap

ear
o'lap

Stag's   Head

Stag's Ears

o'lap

Antler

o'lap   o'lap

overlap

overlap

Tudor Rose
(centre)

Tudor Rose

(main piece)

Heraldic Devices

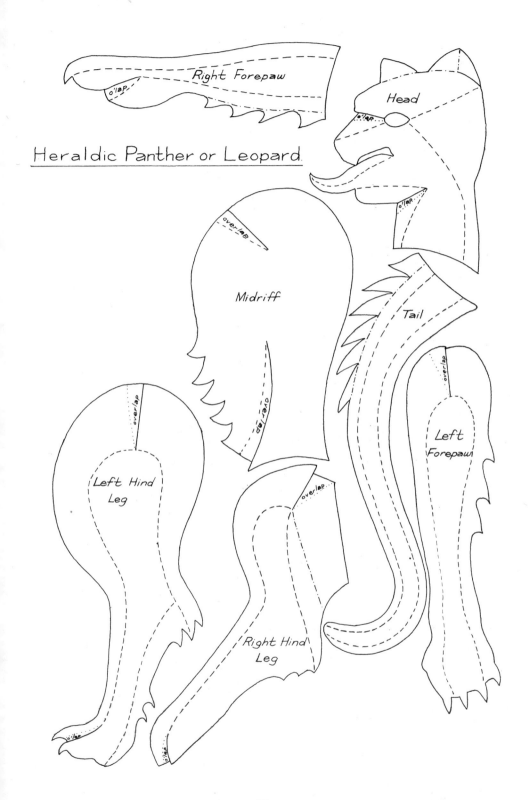

Right Forepaw

Heraldic Panther or Leopard

Head

Midriff

Tail

Left Hind Leg

Right Hind Leg

Left Forepaw

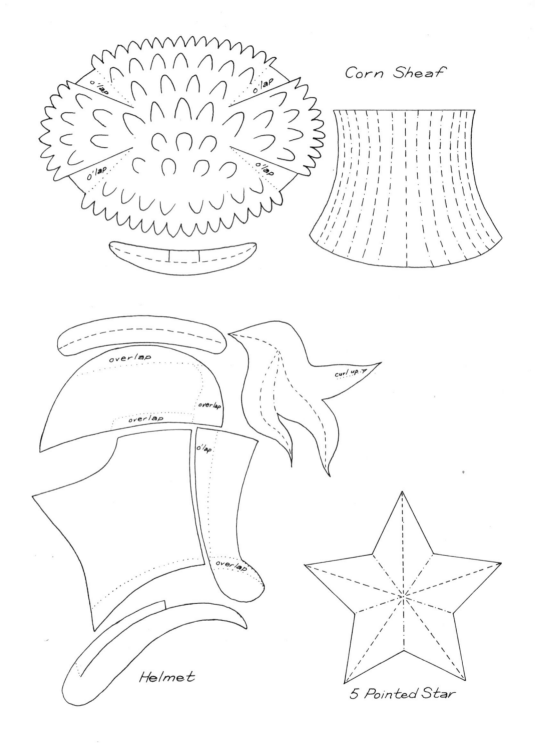

Corn Sheaf

overlap

overlap

overlap

o'lap

overlap

curl up.↗

Helmet

5 Pointed Star

32

The Helmet, Corn Sheaf and Five-pointed Stars. Heraldic devices in relief, made in 'Fabriano' paper and mounted on board. The helmet is painted with gold lacquer and p.v.a. paint. The frame, made to the design for the trapeziform box in Chapter 6, is sprayed with p.v.c. paint.

4 Free-Standing Figures

A free-standing figure is a considerable advance upon pictorial relief sculpture, for where the latter is viewed from the front only, a free-standing figure must be capable of presenting a satisfactory aspect, and hopefully a pleasing one, to every possible viewpoint in three dimensions. Having no backing-board to support it, a free-standing figure must be designed from the start with sufficient strength to support itself. It may also be desirable for its weight to be distributed in balance, so that it will not fall over. This is a problem which can be overcome at a later stage, by glueing the structure to a base, but adequate strength has to be designed and built into the structure itself. Some additional strength can be added to the surface later, by applying paint, varnish or a variety of other similar substances, but the process of applying such surface treatment often has a temporary weakening effect, due to the paper absorbing the liquid in which the pigment is suspended, and until this dries out, the surface can be quite 'flabby'. It is useless, therefore, to rely upon the application of later surface treatment to provide adequate supporting strength for a sculpture; it is more likely to provoke complete collapse.

Generally the best way to provide adequate strength is to build the sculpture upon the simplest possible basic structure that will suit the purpose. The commonest and most useful basic structures are the cone, the cylinder and the tetrahedron or pyramid, upon which many variations and combinations can be based. The strength of the Three Kings, shown on page 37 lies entirely in the basic cone, upon which each of them is built. The remainder of their appearance is mere superimposition.

Designing a successful sculpture is a process which requires individuality and aptitude, qualities that can be developed with practice, but not taught. However, certain methods of approach can be suggested which, while not infallible, may help a beginner in the process of developing design skill.

It is best to start with a specific object in mind, with the intention of producing a recognisable representation, but not a model, of something familiar yet still interesting. Look particularly for characteristic features that lend themselves to portrayal in paper, such as angularity, spikes, or long, flowing lines. When considering the overall design, try to break it down in your mind into simple basic outline shapes — circles, triangles and oblongs. It may help to sketch this simplified outline on paper for each of three views: from the front, from the side and from above — as an engineer would sketch, say, front elevation, side elevation and plan. Having done this, one can consider which simple three-dimensional components can be combined to produce the outlines of the sketches. It often happens that two or more possibilities will suit two of the views and the

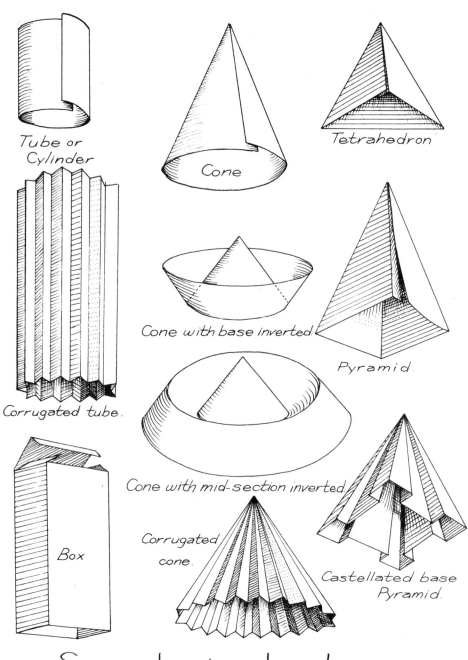

Tube or
Cylinder

Cone

Tetrahedron

Corrugated tube.

Cone with base inverted.

Pyramid.

Cone with mid-section inverted.

Box

Corrugated
cone.

Castellated base
Pyramid.

Some basic structures.

third view is the factor which decides between them. On the rare occasions when a number of possibilities would meet the case, a little experimentation will soon show up the best approach.

One has to accept that the limitations of the medium often make it impossible to reproduce natural shapes with any degree of accuracy. Seek to convey an impression of a shape, rather than strive vainly to copy the shape itself. Paper sculpture, when not purely abstract, inevitably represents nature in a stylised form. This is not the least part of the fascination of paper sculpture and, because of the unavoidable necessity to emphasise certain prominent features when applied to the human shape, stylisation, almost without intent, becomes caricature.

The shapes which seem to give most beginners the greatest difficulty are those which incorporate curves in more than one dimension. Often one has to resolve the problems posed by curves in all three dimensions. A number of different approaches to simulating such shapes are usually available. The possible variations in designing simulations of two problematical shapes which are commonly encountered are illustrated on page 39. The simplest possibility is often the best, but by no means always, for every case is different. You may gain some insight into this crucial matter of design by trying the following projects. These are far from perfect and certainly not beyond criticism, but there is rarely a simple decision between what is right and what is wrong in artistic matters. There are as many ways of representing an owl as there are ways of singing a song, and realism is not necessarily an important criterion. So long as the representation communicates owl-like qualities, further assessment must be subjective.

The Three Kings. Based on cones, these figures are made of cartridge paper and have been sprayed with gold lacquer.

An Angel. Decorated with sections cut from white and gold paper doilies, the angel stands on a brass candlestick.

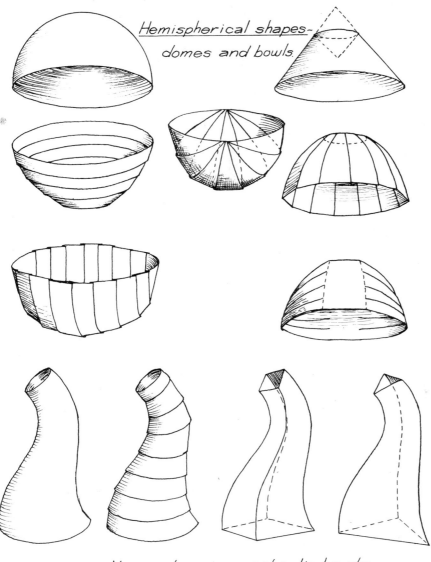

Hemispherical shapes-
domes and bowls.

Horn shapes~ necks, limbs etc.

Design approach to double curves.

The Owl

This figure is built up on a cylinder (Part A) which is tapered towards the feet at the front by cutting this area into parallel strips and overlapping them, which gives an impression of feathers. The same technique is used in the Tail and Wings (Parts E and F) and this has the advantage of producing a very rigid structure very simply. The Top of the Head (Part C) is also very simple, using a shallow cone to represent the real-life dome shape, with the circumference again cut to represent feathers and curled downward. The Face (Part D) is basically another shallow cone with a feathered circumference, but the centre point of the cone has been offset upwards. The Eyes (Part H) are a very prominent feature of any owl, as they are of this one. Again they are formed basically of shallow cones, partially inverted and little more than notched around the circumference to maintain the feathered impression. The Beak (Part G) is uncompromisingly realistic, but note that only the top of an owl's beak is visible, so that is all there is of this one.

A perfectly satisfactory impression of some birds could be conveyed without providing them with any feet at all, but not in this case. An owl lives by using his claws, so they are an important part of true owlishness. These Feet (Part B) bear little resemblance to the talons of a real owl and yet they do portray, in some degree, the cruel clutching power of the genuine article. The figure stands on a simple, log-resembling, T-shaped structure made by joining the centre of a horizontal tube (Part J) to a short vertical one (Part K). To be sure, no ornithologist could identify this bird precisely, but it is unlikely to be mistaken for anything other than an owl.

Assembling the Owl

Cut out and score Parts A and B, raise tabs on B, glue overlap at the back of A to form a cylinder, and then glue front 'feathers' overlapping. Glue front tabs of B inside lower edge of 'feathers' on A. Glue remaining tabs on B around the lower edge of A. Fold talons up and curl the soles, then glue the soles to the talons. Cut out and score C. Curl 'feathers' downward and glue the overlap to form a cone. Glue C on top of A. Cut out D and score as indicated, curl 'feathers' and glue the overlap. Glue D on the front centreline of A. Cut out and score E, curl the 'feathers' slightly and glue them overlapping. Glue E to lower back centreline of A. Cut out and score G, fold and glue tabs to form beak shape. Glue G to centre of D. Cut out and score H pieces. Form carefully along score lines and glue overlaps. Glue H pieces to D each side of, and slightly above, G. Cut out and score F parts, glue 'feathers' overlapping, fold top tabs upward and glue to A. Glue lower tips of front wing 'feathers' down onto Body. Cut out J and K, score K, form into tubular sections and glue overlaps. Fold down tabs on K and glue J centrally to them. When J and K are dry, mount the Owl on top of J with a little glue at the base of the talons and the ends of the outer tail 'feathers'.

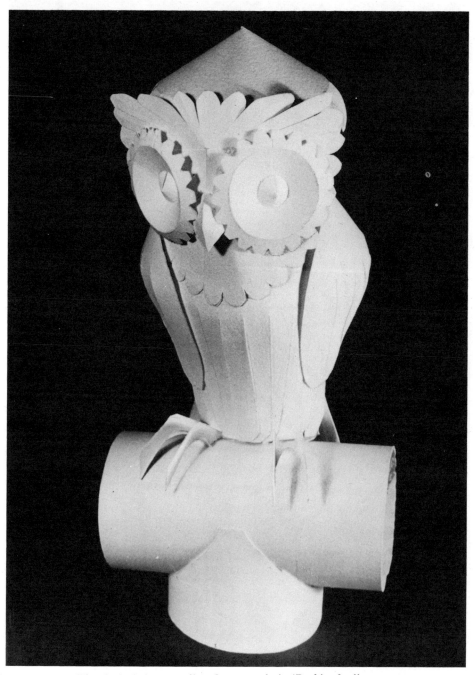

The Owl. A free-standing figure made in 'Bockingford' paper.

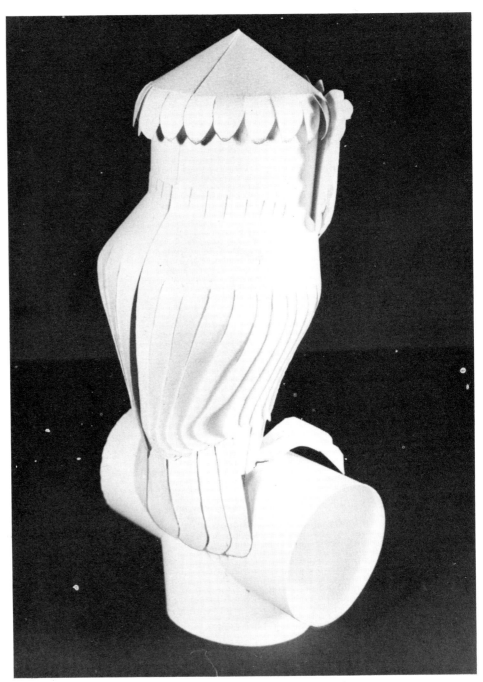

Back view of the Owl.

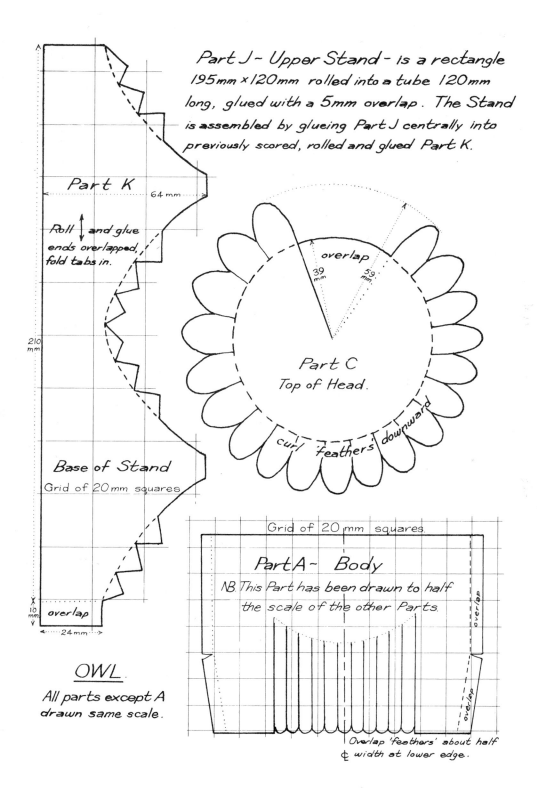

Part J - Upper Stand - is a rectangle 195mm × 120mm rolled into a tube 120mm long, glued with a 5mm overlap. The Stand is assembled by glueing Part J centrally into previously scored, rolled and glued Part K.

Part K

64 mm

Roll and glue ends overlapped, fold tabs in.

210 mm

overlap

39 mm

59 mm

Part C
Top of Head.

curl 'feathers' downward

Base of Stand
Grid of 20mm squares

10 mm

overlap

24 mm

OWL.

All parts except A drawn same scale.

Grid of 20 mm squares.

Part A ~ Body
NB. This Part has been drawn to half the scale of the other Parts.

overlap

overlap

Overlap 'feathers' about half
₵ width at lower edge.

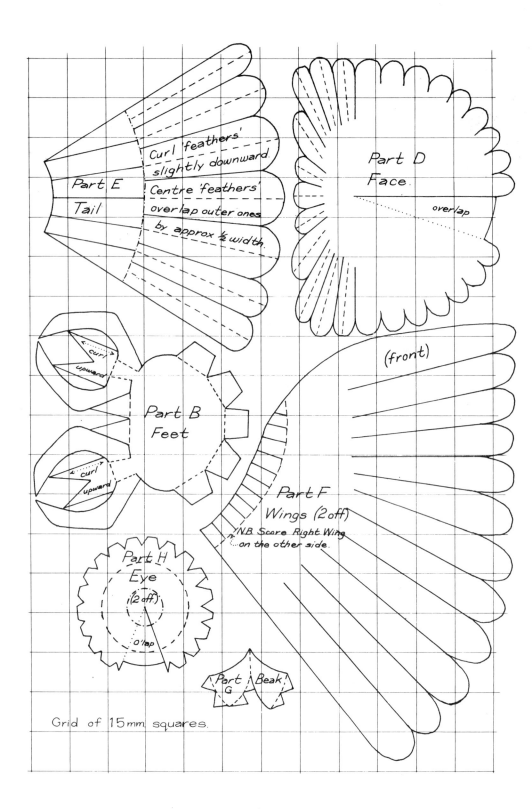

Part E
Tail

Curl 'feathers'
slightly downward.
Centre 'feathers'
overlap outer ones
by approx ½ width.

Part D
Face.

overlap

(front)

Part B
Feet

curl
upward

curl
upward

Part F
Wings (2 off)

N.B. Score Right Wing
on the other side.

Part H
Eye
(2 off.)

o'lap

Part Beak
G

Grid of 15 mm. squares.

The Dragon

This figure is based upon an elongated box section, forming the body; the head and most of the neck being of a four-sided section, and the upper neck narrowing to a short length of triangular section with a crest. The eyes and nostrils are indicated by narrow conical sections glued in place. The mane or crest along neck and body is a silhouette, held vertically in position by tabs folded and glued each side alternately. The tail is formed of tapering tubes, the rear end of each cut obliquely, with the following tube's leading end glued inside. The tail ends in two flat arrow-shaped pieces glued together and with a fold around the final tube. The forelegs are straight tubes; the hindlegs are also tubes, but cut in two obliquely, the lower section inserted and glued into the upper to form a joint. The feet are star-shaped pieces, folded alternately, with tabs folded and glued together underneath at the toes, and more tabs folded down and glued to the lower end of the legs at the ankles. All the legs are held in place by shoulder and haunch pieces, rolled over at the top, flat at front and back, the upper end of the legs being glued between, and with tabs folded inward and glued to the body. The body, shoulders and haunches have V-shaped notches cut in their surfaces, the points being lifted outwards to represent scales. The horns are very thin cones, with tabs at the bases for glueing in position. The forked tongue is a suitably shaped and slightly curled piece, glued into the lower front part of the head, there being no formal mouth. The smoke whorls are made from two small circles of paper, cut with scissors into narrow spirals, working from the circumference inward towards the centre, and glued in place with the outer end of each spiral in a nostril.

Assembling the Dragon

Cut out, score and fold the five body pieces (two Sides, Top, Underside Front and Rear), then cut and raise the 'scales'. Glue together Sides and Undersides. Insert and glue in position Top of Body. Cut out, score and fold Top of Head, and glue in position. Cut out, score and fold Mane and glue in position. Cut out and assemble all Leg pieces, but not Feet. Cut out, score, fold and roll Shoulders and Haunches, remembering to cut and raise the 'scales'. Glue Shoulders to Forelegs and Haunches to Hindlegs, ensuring that they are at the correct angle, by offering up one at a time to the Body before the glue has set, and adjusting as necessary. Leave for the glue to set hard whilst cutting out, rolling and assembling all Tail pieces. The Tail may be assembled complete and then glued on to the Body, or it may be assembled piece by piece in position on the Body. When the Leg assemblies are firmly set, glue them in position on the Body, first glueing both Hindlegs and then both Forelegs, making sure that the Body is held upright and does not lean to one side or the other. (Note that the weight of the whole figure is supported on the leg tubes, the feet merely adding stability.) Cut out, score and fold the Feet and glue them in position. Cut out, score and fold the Wings and glue them in position. Finally the Eyes, Nostrils, Horns and Ears are cut out, prepared and glued into position. The tongue and smoke whorls are optional — see the description above if you want to add them.

This figure looks handsome sprayed with gold or a metallic green paint, but BE CAREFUL, and spray several thin coats, allowing drying time in between, or you may find the paint dissolving the glue, with disastrous results. If in doubt, experiment by spraying a few glued-together offcuts first.

The Dragon. A free-standing figure made in 'Fabriano' paper.

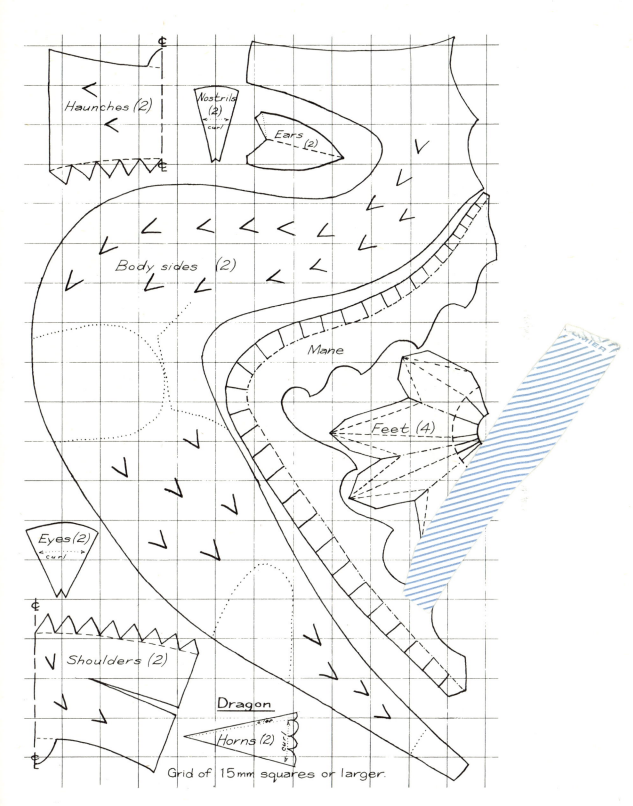

Haunches (2)

Nostrils (2)
curl

Ears (2)

Body sides (2)

Mane

Feet (4)

Eyes (2)
curl

Shoulders (2)

Dragon

Horns (2)
curl

Grid of 15mm squares or larger.

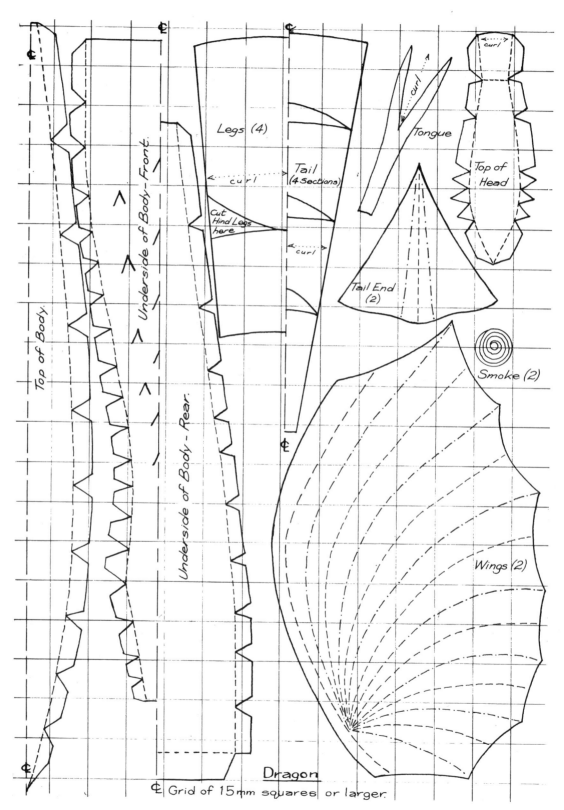

Top of Body.

Underside of Body-Front.

Underside of Body - Rear.

Legs (4)

curl

Cut
Hind Legs
here

Tail
(4 Sections)

curl

Tail End
(2)

Tongue

curl

Top of
Head

curl

Smoke (2)

Wings (2)

Dragon

Grid of 15 mm squares or larger.

The Horse

Although the photograph on page 50 shows this figure with saddle and harness, ready for the mounted Knight (see page 53), it may be made as a separate figure, without harness, if preferred. It is also possible to alter and adjust the horse's pose, by cutting the legs where indicated on the drawing, and assembling them in different attitudes. In some other poses, balance can be a problem, in which case it may be necessary to glue the hooves to a base made from mounting board. It is advisable to keep at least three hooves on the 'ground' otherwise additional support, such as wires passing from a base into and up the legs, will have to be devised. The Horse's Body is a simple tapering tube, to the narrower end of which the box-section Hindquarters are glued. The Head is also basically a tapering rectangular box, open underneath. The top part of each Hind Leg is formed into a shallow cone and glued to the Hindquarters. All of the remaining major pieces — Legs, Chest and Neck — are U-shaped sections. In the case of the Chest, the 'legs' of the U are glued to the sides at the wide end of the Body tube. The Legs and Neck are formed by pinching the U sections closed and glueing them at intervals. The Eyes and Ears are very similar to those of the Dragon, and the Tail is really a roll, cut for most of its length into several parallel strips. The Mane is not included in the drawing, but is easily made by tracing the curve of the Neck onto two pieces of paper and cutting these in thin strips downward from the curves, which are then glued to the Neck.

Assembling the Horse

Cut out, roll and glue the Body. Cut out, score and form the Hindquarters, and glue them to the narrow end of the Body (note that the overlap of the Body should be positioned downwards). Cut out, score and form the Chest and Neck piece. The sides of the Chest are tucked *inside* the Body tube's wide end and glued in position. The lower corners of the Neck are then glued to the *outside* of the Body, adjusted so that the angle at which the neck is held suits the intended pose. Glue together the edges along the top of the Neck, using clothes pegs or paper clips to hold them together while the glue sets. Cut out, score and fold the Head, and glue it in shape. When it is dry, glue it in position on the Neck, adjusting the angle to suit the intended pose.

Cut out, roll and glue all four Legs as four complete pieces. The easiest way of forming and glueing the Legs is to do this around a piece of thin dowelling, tube or rod of about 6 mm ($\frac{1}{4}$ in.) diameter, which can be removed when the glue has set. Use clothes pegs or paper clips to hold the glued areas together while the glue dries. Now decide which Leg joints are to be bent and cut across the appropriate Legs at the indicated points with scissors. This will slightly distort the sectional shape, but it can be restored very easily. Glue the bent joints together by inserting the lower section of Leg into the upper. A minimal amount of trimming may be required, but try to reduce the length of each limb as little as possible. Glue the Legs into position, first one side and then the other.

Note that the Hind Legs are secured at the front and top circumferential edges, the front edges being glued to the Body, whilst the top edges extend over and are glued down onto the sides of the upper surface of the Hindquarters. The Eyes, Ears and Tail can now be cut out, formed and glued into position. Finally the Mane pieces (not included in the drawing, but described above) must be produced and glued in place. Either as a part of the Mane, or as a small separate piece, do not forget that a forelock should extend forward between the Ears and over the forehead. This forelock is clearly visible in the photograph of the mounted Knight.

If you wish to proceed with saddle and harness, the Saddle components are drawn on page 54. The Saddlebows are semi-circular and have tabs which are folded and glued to the underside of the Saddle piece. A saddlecloth, of dimensions to suit the scale of the drawing, is glued across the horse's back first, and the completed Saddle is then glued on top of the saddlecloth. The lower edges of the saddlecloth and reins, also the rear edges of the stirrup leathers, may be cut with pinking shears, to simulate fringing, as are those in the photographs. The actual harness straps, reins and stirrup leathers are not drawn, as these are simply strips which are glued in place. Note that the upper ends of the stirrup leathers are pushed up and glued underneath the Saddle at the appropriate point. Where the harness straps meet, at the horse's mouth and cheeks, small discs are positioned, covering the joins. The rider's end of the reins may be folded and glued to the front saddlebow.

The Horse. A free-standing figure made in 'Fabriano' paper.

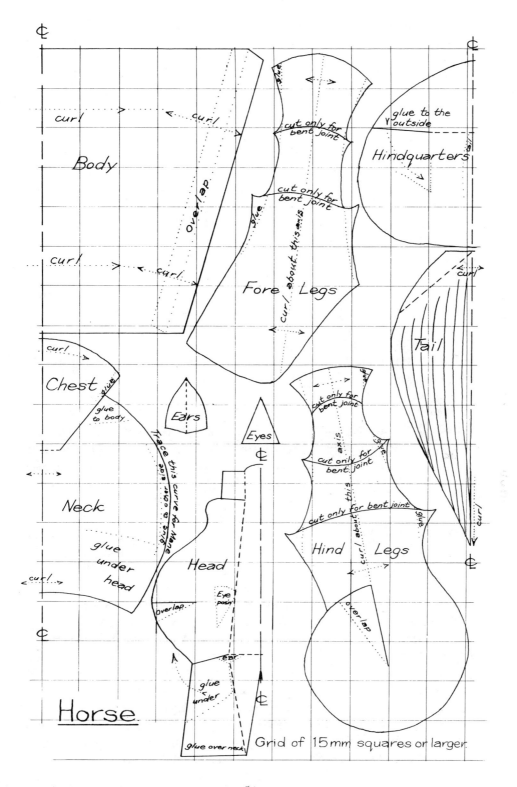

curl

curl

Body

glue

cut only for
bent joint

glue to the
outside

Hindquarters

overlap

curl

curl

cut only for
bent joint

glue

curl about this axis

Fore Legs

Tail

curl

curl

Chest

glue

glue
to body

Ears

Eyes

cut only for
bent joint

cut only for
bent joint

cut only for bent joint

glue

curl

Neck

trace this curve for Mane

glue
under
head

Head

Hind   Legs

curl about this axis

curl

curl

Eye
posn

overlap

overlap

ear

glue
under

glue over neck

Grid of 15mm squares or larger

Horse

The Knight in Armour

This figure mainly consists of tubes and cones. Tubes form the Body, Arms and Legs, while cones form the Helmet, Collar and Flare at the hips. Over the Body tube a Tabard is glued, and the Helmet, formed of two cone shapes, the points of which are slightly offset from their centres, is fixed on top of the Tabard by means of a shallow conical Collar. The slightly conical flared piece indicating the hips provides, and also conveniently hides, the connection of the Upper Legs. The Knight carries a Shield, fixed to the left Arm with a strip on the back (not drawn). In the photographs the mounted Knight is shown armed with a lance (not drawn), but he could equally well be equipped with a sword or battle-axe, and stand on his own feet, if glued to a base, as sit on a horse.

Assembling the Knight

Cut out, roll and glue the Body. Cut out and roll the Tabard. Cut out and glue the overlap of the Flare piece, then glue this over the narrower end of the Body tube, with both overlaps positioned at the back. Glue the Tabard well down over the Body tube, so that the ends overlap the Flare to about half its depth. Cut out and glue the overlap of the Collar, then glue it in position on the Tabard, with the overlap at the back, so that the whole of its lower circumference fits snugly to the top of the Tabard. Cut out and form the Helmet lower half and top pieces, and glue them together, overlaps at the back. They should fit together snugly from side to side around the back, leaving an open gap at the front. Cut out and curl the Visor and glue it over the open gap at the front of the Helmet, with a small disc at each end to represent the Visor's pivots. Cut out and form the pieces of each Arm in turn, glueing the wider part of each lower arm inside the elbow of the upper arm. The upper arms will probably need to be trimmed at the elbows to accept the forearms at the correct angle, and again at the shoulders to make the glued joints beneath the Tabard as neat as possible. Glue the left Arm in position, bent approximately at right angles, so that the Shield will rest on it without obstruction. Before fixing the Right Arm, it is necessary to decide upon and make the weapon which it is to hold, so that the arm can be correctly positioned. The Gauntlets can be cut out, curled and tucked into the ends of the Arms at any convenient stage, but it is easier to make them look natural if they are only glued into position once the arms have been fixed. Now cut out, roll and glue the overlaps on both Legs. How the knee joint is cut and fixed will depend upon the figure's intended pose, whether sitting or standing, and some trimming may be necessary at the tops of the upper legs to produce a neat join. The Boots, having been cut out and curled across the tops, are formed by glueing together the two faces of the heels, not overlapping them as might be imagined, but aligning their edges. The lower Leg pieces are notched at the ankles to overlap the Boots, which are glued inside them. Finally cut out, form and glue into position the Elbow Guards, Helmet Band and Plumes. A short strip is needed to secure the Shield to the left arm. The arm passes between the

Shield and the strip, which is glued to the back of the Shield above and below it. It is not necessary to glue the Shield to the left arm, but it may be convenient to do so. The manufacture of a weapon or weapons for the Knight is left to your own ingenuity. The lance is very simple to make, although considerable care is needed to roll such a thin cone. The design of a sword or a battleaxe should be well within the capability of anyone able to make the Knight or his horse.

The Knight in Armour, made in 'Fabriano' paper.

The Knight in Armour, mounted on the Horse.

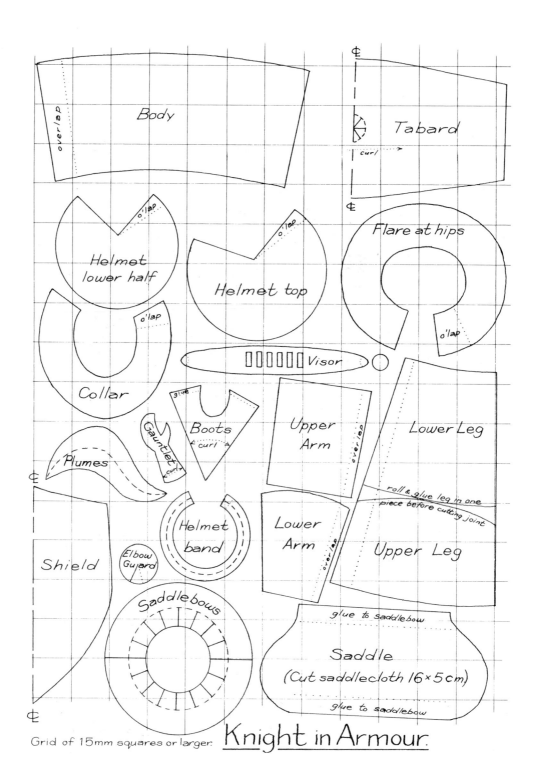

Body

Tabard

∉

curl

Helmet lower half

o'lap

Helmet top

o'lap

Flare at hips

o'lap

Collar

o'lap

Visor

Upper Arm

overlap

Lower Leg

Plumes

Gauntlet
curl

Boots
curl

glue

Lower Arm

overlap

roll & glue leg in one piece before cutting joint

Upper Leg

∉

Shield

Elbow Guard

Helmet band

∉

Saddlebows

glue to saddlebow

Saddle
(Cut saddlecloth 16 × 5 cm)

glue to saddlebow

Grid of 15mm squares or larger.

Knight in Armour.

St. George and the Dragon.

5 Practical Uses for Paper Sculpture

The first part of this book has dealt with paper sculpture primarily as a creative art form — the function for which it is best known. However, the following pages are intended to show that the techniques of paper sculpture can be used in many more practical ways.

Several of the designs which follow are meant for everyday use and some may need to withstand considerable wear and tear in a utilitarian role. In such circumstances it is right to ask whether paper is a suitable material for the purpose. In some cases it will be perfectly satisfactory, for instance in making frames for pictures or photographs which are not intended or expected to encounter much knocking about. For this purpose 200 gsm cartridge paper is excellent; given a couple of coats of paint it will last indefinitely and can be kept just as clean as any wooden frame. In other circumstances, for toys or bookends for example, paper needs all the protection it can get. There are several effective ways of improving the wearing qualities and thus extending the life of articles made from paper, whether these are items of purely artistic paper sculpture or something more mundane.

Paint, Lacquer and Varnish

There are innumerable varieties of paint readily available in the shops and nearly all of them can be applied to paper, but some are more suitable than others. In general it is preferable to use plastic paints; they are more flexible than the traditional oil or spirit based pigmented paints which tend to be rather brittle. The normal household emulsion paints are excellent since they are very flexible, tough and washable, but, at the time of writing, only matt, eggshell or silk finish can be achieved, so for a high gloss one must look elsewhere. Polyurethane paint, lacquer and varnish are widely available in a variety of colours with a high gloss finish. These produce a very hard and strong protective coat, which is also flexible and adds considerably to the structural strength of a paper product. Some polyurethane paints and clear varnishes are obtainable in an aerosol spray pack, which can be most convenient for some purposes, although rather expensive. Another kind of paint, available in aerosol spray cans, is sold for refurbishing p.v.c. upholstery, particularly in motor cars, but it has proved to be a good choice for paper also. The frames around the leopard and stag's head, shown in Chapter 6 were sprayed with this p.v.c. paint, in a metallic silvery green shade, and have withstood considerably more abuse than could be expected in normal domestic circumstances.

Chemical resins, of the type normally used with glass fibre reinforcement, also can be used to impart greatly increased strength to a paper structure, but do be sure to follow the manufacturer's instructions for use carefully, as there are usually important precautions to be taken in handling this material.

For some purposes it may be desirable to add surface texture to a paper structure, as on the animal masks in Chapter 7 for instance. This can be done by applying a cement wash, such as Snowcem, mixed to a fairly thick consistency. The application of an undercoat of emulsion before the cement wash is helpful in that it prevents the water in the cement wash being absorbed by the paper, thus causing distortion and 'flabbiness'. One must remember, however, that such cement washes dry into a very hard granular coat which is not flexible and will crack quite easily if the surface to which they have been applied is flexed. Some new and more flexible preparations, capable of forming a textured surface, have been advertised recently for interior decoration, and these may be found more suitable than cement wash for use on paper articles.

Some books about paper sculpture advise painting the paper before making the sculpture. This advice is not always helpful, however, and can produce as many problems as it solves. Much depends upon the kind of paint being used and the means available for its application. The advantage of painting the paper before cutting and construction lies mainly in the fact that paint can be applied more easily to a flat sheet, compared with a three-dimensional object which is often complicated by fragile and convoluted detail. The disadvantages of painting in advance include:

1. the risk that the glue and the paint may prove incompatible, so that the glue will not set properly or may cause discolouration or blistering of the paint.
2. if a high gloss is required, the surface may be damaged accidentally all too easily during construction.
3. in cutting the paper one must also cut the paint, thus exposing unpainted edges.
4. the structural strength of the whole product can be enhanced by painting after construction, whereas additional stresses may be induced by having painted the material in advance, and the paint on curved surfaces may crack or craze.
5. any minor blemishes caused during construction are likely to show clearly on paintwork done in advance, whereas they will often be camouflaged or completely obliterated by paint applied afterwards.

The two principal dangers associated with painting after construction are, first, the risk that the paint may dissolve the glue and, second, the risk of causing accidental damage with a paintbrush. A further problem in using a paintbrush at this stage may be the difficulty in reaching inaccessible but visible nooks and crannies.

The first danger can be avoided by taking the trouble to select a paint which either will not dissolve the glue, or may be applied over a protective undercoat sealing the glue against such attack. The second and its associated dangers, stemming from the use of a paintbrush, can be avoided completely by not using a paintbrush at all and spraying the paint on instead. The use of aerosol paints has been mentioned already, and these are perfectly satisfactory, provided that they are used with care, laying the paint on in a series of thin coats, with drying time allowed between them, rather than attempting complete coverage in one coat. This also helps to avoid the risk of dissolving glue, because it is not the paint which acts as the offending solvent, but the spirit in which it is suspended, and which evaporates off very quickly from a thinly sprayed coat. The ideal tool for applying paint to paper sculpture is the artist's air-brush, but air-brushes are expensive. A cheaper alternative has become available recently, intended for modelling enthusiasts and sold through shops which cater for them; it is marketed in Great Britain by Humbrol, and combines the convenience of replaceable aerosol propellant and the flexibility of a small spraygun, capable of applying most types of paint in quite small quantities.

Plastic Self-Adhesive Film

There are many kinds and brands of plastic films, treated with a self-adhesive backing and available in various widths, qualities, designs and textures; all are well suited to the purpose of providing a decorative, washable and abrasion resistant surface on paper products. A good example of the advantageous use of this type of material is provided by the chess board shown in the photograph on page 102. The board itself is made from interwoven strips of card, painted with silver and copper-coloured metallic lacquer. This looked very effective, but seemed unlikely to withstand much wear and tear. The problem was solved by applying a transparent self-adhesive plastic film over the whole surface. The frame around the edge of the chess board was made using the design for a triangular box-section frame in Chapter 6 and was covered with a plastic self-adhesive film giving the appearance of light oak. The material was used so that the wood grain pattern runs the full length of each side, being carefully cut at the corners to simulate mitred joints.

In situations requiring transparency, bright appearance, flexibility, abrasion resistance and washability these self-adhesive plastic films are excellent, but they add little to structural strength, and may even detract from it because of their relative weight per unit area.

Other Plastic Products and Alternatives to Paper

The techniques described and the designs provided in this book should not be regarded as exclusively applicable to paper and card. Most of them can be applied to many other materials, which are available in thin, flexible sheet form. Indeed, for some purposes, materials other than paper may be more suitable. For instance there are several kinds of translucent, coloured and patterned materials made specifically for the purpose of producing lampshades and, in that role, they are preferable to paper as thay are non-inflammable and heat resistant, but the techniques for shaping and forming paper are equally applicable to most, if not all, lampshade materials.

The simple two-dimensional constructional toys featured in Chapter 8 can be made from paper or card, but the wear and tear likely to be suffered by any toy is such that no ordinary paper can be expected to last very long without substantial protection. Almost any kind of plastic sheet will do better for this purpose, and plastic cartons, normally thrown away, will often provide excellent material. They can be cut with strong scissors or a craft knife, to form various components of toys or games. The chess men in Chapter 8 could be made almost as easily from old plastic washing-up liquid bottles as from paper. The only problem that may arise in using plastic is that of finding the right glue; some plastics are almost impossible to glue and others dissolve with a mere whiff of glue, but many take quite happily to products such as Uhu or Bostik. There are, of course, special glues available for most plastics, such as that sold for assembling the plastic model kits, or another for joining plastic drainpipe and guttering. One word of warning must be added about inflammable plastics such as acrylics; some of these flare up very easily and are not at all suitable for use as toy components or domestic articles. If you are in any doubt about a material, cut a little piece off one corner, place it in a clear area inside something safe, such as a tin lid, and apply a match to it: if it burns easily, avoid it.

The two-dimensional toys in Chapter 8 require no glue, but the more different colours they can be produced in, the better toys they become. Paint is not really the answer. For one thing, not all paints are suitable for use on toys, where non-toxic and non-inflammable products are essential; also even the best paints become scratched and chipped in time. Plastic sheet, which is integrally coloured, as brightly as possible, provides the best material and there are at least two brands of p.v.c. sheet, about half a millimetre thick, available in Britain in a wide range of bright colours, which are well suited to this purpose. One, made by ICI Ltd., is known as 'Darvic'; the other, made by Bakelite Xylonite Ltd., is known as 'Cobex'.

Some paper sculpture techniques can be applied to metal sheet and foils, particularly the softer ones, such as copper, aluminium and pewter; these can be cut, folded and curled, in much the same way as paper. Problems arise when they have to be glued, however. Although epoxy resin glues can be quite effective for this purpose, they are relatively expensive and set slowly. Nevertheless, for some purposes, the use of metal sheet or foil alongside or in conjunction with paper, card or plastic sheet may be well worth considering.

Finally one must not overlook the use of fabrics with paper to provide a decorative surface and protection against abrasion and also, in some circumstances, to increase structural strength. Many light cotton fabrics can be pasted onto paper using wallpaper paste, before cutting for construction. Heavier materials, such as linen, velvet and leather for instance, need something stronger than wallpaper paste, and here a latex adhesive, such as 'Copydex', is appropriate. This technique is particularly suitable for domestic articles, such as pot holders, lampshades and frames, which can be matched to curtains and upholstery. Bear in mind during construction that the fabric should appear on the outside. This can produce problems when scoring on the outer surface and is one of the rare occasions when it may be better to score on the inside of a fold, rather than cut through the fabric on the outside. Since the fabric will provide an adequate hinge by itself, the score on the inside can be much deeper than normal, thus ensuring a crisp fold despite the score being on the wrong side.

6 Frames

One of the most valuable practical uses of paper sculpture is in providing frames for pictures, photographs, collages and relief sculpture. The possible variations on this theme are endless and frames can be as large or small, as plain or ornate as the available materials and one's own sense of taste dictate. A number of different designs are provided here, from a simple round frame to a fairly complicated interlocking system.

A round frame can be made in basically the same way as one of the medallions previously encountered in Chapter 3, with the centre removed and an annulus added to close the section at the back. To attach the annulus to the front of the frame section, folded tabs are glued inside. These tabs could be on the frame front, but are better positioned around the inner and outer circumference of the annulus. The frame front can then be made to overlap them as required.

The most difficult part of producing a satisfactory rectangular frame is the formation of strong, neat corners. If a simple rectangular box section is acceptable, the solution is relatively straightforward, but normally picture frames are made to slope from the outer edge inwards towards the picture, forming a triangular or trapeziform section. Designing a clean right-angled change of direction at the corners requires careful thought and often some experiment as well.

The more complicated the frame or architrave section becomes, the more difficult are the problems in forming satisfactory corners. Eventually the only solution lies in making the corners as separate pieces, and this is what has been done in the design for the Interlocking Picture Framing System. The basic architrave section, Type A, is a simple triangle, onto which, in the Type B section, a triangular 'moulding' has been added. By cutting into this 'moulding' section and by scoring and folding parts of it inwards, as well as outwards, an enormous number of design variations are possible, of which a mere dozen have been illustrated. The corner pieces are strong, being doubled in thickness at the back, and they allow the ends of the architrave pieces forming the sides of the frame to be push-fitted into them with an ample overlap. This allows one to assemble and dismantle frames for exhibition work and interim storage, if so desired. For permanency the assembly would be glued together.

Paper frames are not, as a rule, sufficiently substantial to carry glass. However, several quite satisfactory alternatives to glass are widely available. Depending upon the purpose for which the frame is intended, a choice can be made from clear, transparent acrylic or p.v.c. sheet, in thicknesses from about 3 mm, when it is quite rigid, down to very flexible sheet, only a fraction of a millimetre thick. Ordinary transparent polyethylene film may be a perfectly satisfactory choice in some circumstances.

The simplest method of permanently applying a paper frame to a picture is, of course, just to stick it on with glue or a double-sided self-adhesive tape. Ordinary wooden picture frames are secured to backing-boards with pins or tacks, but a different method must be used with a paper frame if it is to be made so that the picture in it can be changed. Probably the most satisfactory method of securing a paper frame to a backing-board, with the picture in between, of course, is to fix a number of brass bifurcated paper clips at intervals around the back of the frame. Make sure that the heads of the clips are inside the frame section and their points are towards the backing-board, which should have holes punched to correspond with the positions of the clips. The points of the paper clips can be passed through the backing-board and opened out flat, in the usual way, to secure the frame, picture and backing-board together. Two important points have to be remembered in making such a frame; the first is that the heads of the paper clips must be inside the frame when it is made — they cannot be put in afterwards — and the second essential is that the heads must be secured inside the frames with a drop of glue, a piece of adhesive tape, or a disc of glued paper over the head, so that the clips cannot fall back inside the frame.

In order to frame and protect permanently a piece of relief sculpture, the frame must be deep enough below the transparent sheet to accommodate the depth of the sculpture in front of the backing-board. To produce an architrave section of a suitable shape for such a frame in paper is possible, but the corners become very complex indeed. The best solution to this problem is to produce two separate frames, one lying above the other. The lower frame is a simple box section, glued to the backing-board and acting as a distance-piece to hold the transparent protective plastic clear of the relief sculpture. The upper frame, of triangular or trapeziform section, provides the decorative finish and secures the transparent sheet from above. A strip, forming a flange, runs all the way around the outside edge of the frame, keeping the upper part in place above the lower and hiding the join. Since the frame has been made for the express purpose of protecting a particular piece of relief sculpture, it is best to glue all the parts together permanently.

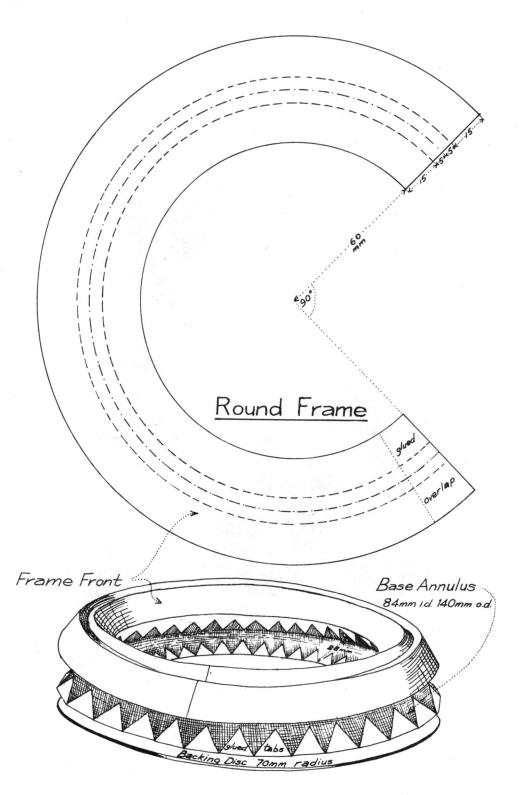

Round Frame

60 mm

90°

·15 ·15 ·5·5·5· ·15

glued

overlap

Frame Front

Base Annulus
84mm i.d. 140mm o.d.

glued tabs

Backing Disc 70mm radius

Composite Deep Frame. Triangular and square box sections, made in 200 gsm cartridge paper, and glazed with rigid clear p.v.c.

Oval Tesselated Composite Deep Frame. Made in 200 gsm cartridge paper, sprayed with p.v.c. paint and glazed with clear rigid p.v.c., this frame combines several of the techniques covered in Chapter 6.

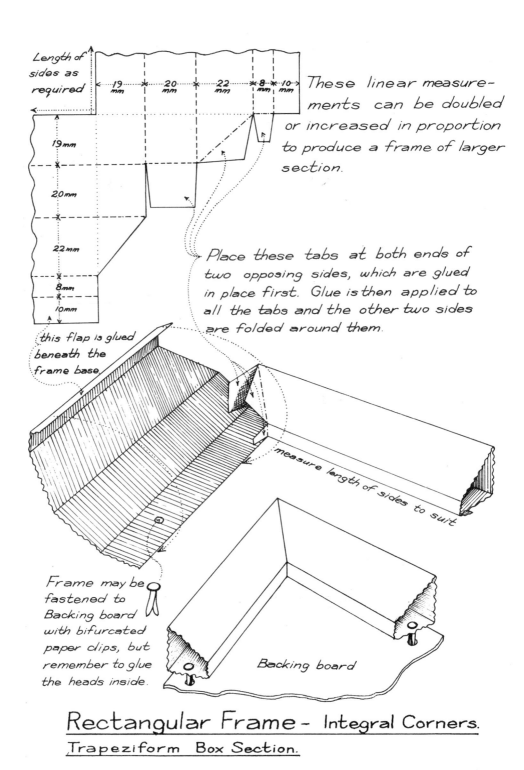

Length of sides as required

19 mm   20 mm   22 mm   8 mm   10 mm

These linear measurements can be doubled or increased in proportion to produce a frame of larger section.

19mm

20mm

22mm

8mm

10mm

this flap is glued beneath the frame base.

Place these tabs at both ends of two opposing sides, which are glued in place first. Glue is then applied to all the tabs and the other two sides are folded around them.

measure length of sides to suit

Frame may be fastened to Backing board with bifurcated paper clips, but remember to glue the heads inside.

Backing board

Rectangular Frame - Integral Corners.
Trapeziform Box Section.

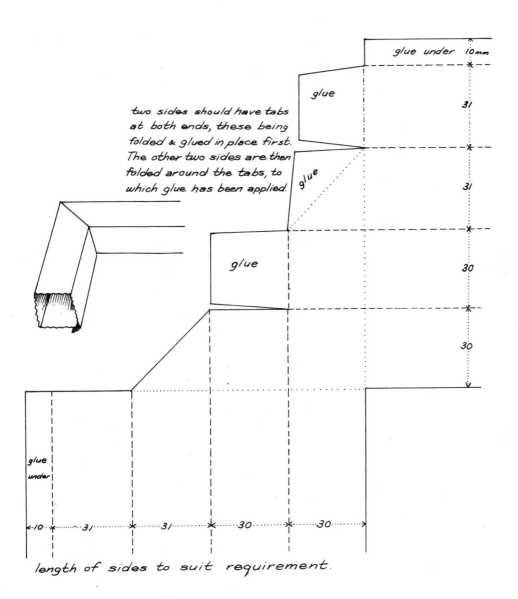

glue under 10mm

31

glue

glue

31

30

two sides should have tabs
at both ends, these being
folded & glued in place first.
The other two sides are then
folded around the tabs, to
which glue has been applied.

glue

30

glue
under

10 — 31 — 31 — 30 — 30

length of sides to suit requirement.

Corner for a Square Box Section Frame.

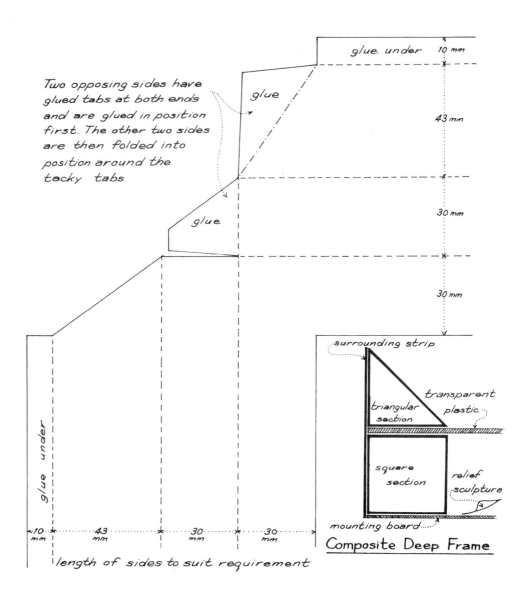

Two opposing sides have glued tabs at both ends and are glued in position first. The other two sides are then folded into position around the tacky tabs.

glue under   10 mm

glue

43 mm

30 mm

30 mm

glue

glue under

←10 mm→   43 mm   30 mm   30 mm

length of sides to suit requirement

surrounding strip

triangular section

transparent plastic

square section

relief sculpture

mounting board

Composite Deep Frame

Corner of Triangular Box Section Frame.

This will fit above the Square Section Frame to form a deep frame for protective glazing over relief sculpture.

The Interlocking Framing System. Each side of the frame has two different 'moulding' designs.

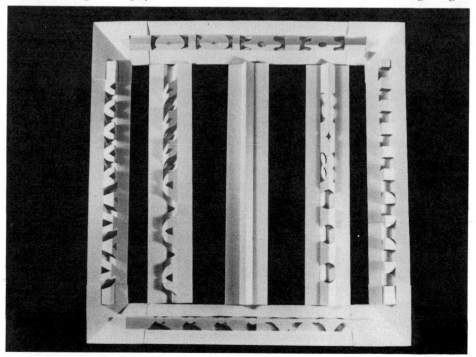

The Interlocking Framing System. Some ideas for different 'moulding' designs.

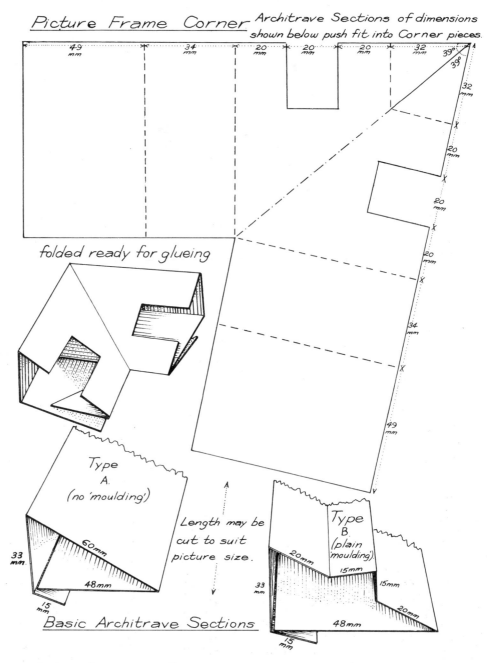

Picture Frame Corner

Architrave Sections of dimensions shown below push fit into Corner pieces.

49 mm   34 mm   20 mm   20 mm   20 mm   32 mm   39°
39°
32 mm
20 mm
20 mm
20 mm
34 mm
49 mm

folded ready for glueing

Type A. (no 'moulding')

60mm

33 mm

48mm

15 mm

Length may be cut to suit picture size.

Type B. (plain moulding)

20mm

15mm

15mm

33 mm

48mm

20mm

15 mm

Basic Architrave Sections

Interlocking Picture Framing System.

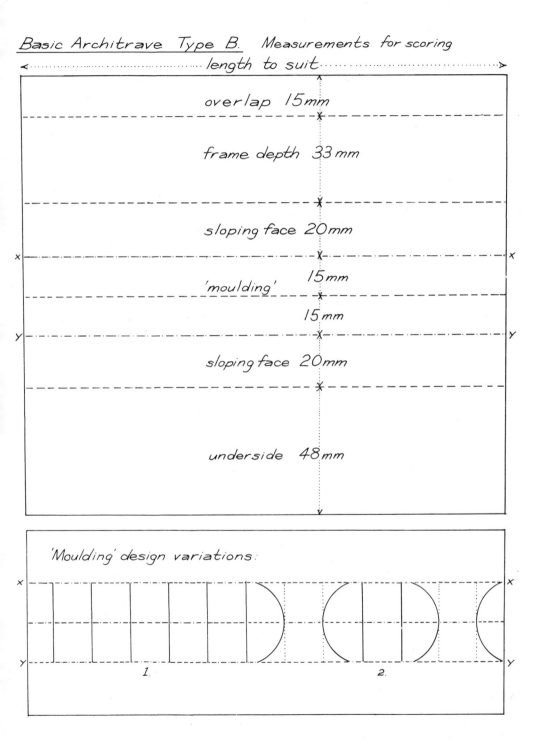

Basic Architrave Type B.   Measurements for scoring

← ·················· length to suit ·················· →

overlap 15mm

frame depth 33mm

sloping face 20mm

'moulding' 15mm

15mm

sloping face 20mm

underside 48mm

'Moulding' design variations:

1.   2.

3.

4.

5.

6.

7.

8.

9.

10.

11.

12.

Architrave 'Moulding' Design Variations.

7 'Props' for Stage and Carnival

The director of an amateur theatrical event of any kind, be it pageant, fête or formal drama, rarely can afford to buy or hire all the scenery, costumes and other 'props' that he or she would like. The techniques of paper sculpture can be a great help in providing the required illusion at a relatively insignificant cost.

Most kinds of hats and helmets can be made from heavy (200 gsm) paper or card for, in general, they consist of a conical base with a brim, and perhaps a crown, added. The variations mainly occur in the height and taper of the cone, which becomes a cylinder in the case of a top hat, and in the width and curl of the brim. The helmet of a modern soldier is not a good subject, being intentionally all smooth curves, but old-fashioned helmets, before the days of heavy presses, can be fairly simple to reproduce in paper. The helmet of the Knight in Armour, shown in Chapter 4, can be produced on a larger scale, for instance.

A basic ladies' bonnet is simple enough, and a suitable design is provided here. This can be altered in various ways and can be decorated with paper flowers, birds, ribbon, bows, sections of paper doilies representing lace, and frills of crêpe paper so as to outshine the most fanciful Ascot creation.

A crown is often needed, whether for a beauty queen or a Shakespearian monarch, and a typical design is shown; numerous variations can be based on this. After spraying the completed crown with gold paint, jewels can be simulated by blobs of glue covered with different coloured glitter of the kind used on Christmas cards.

Animal heads are very expensive to hire, yet they are not difficult to make from paper and card. The head of Tyrannosaurus Rex, originally designed at the request of two small boys in order to frighten the daylights out of parents and small sisters at a school fête, is included here because it is a very straightforward basic shape. With the addition of ears, squaring up the teeth and perhaps reducing the size of the mouth a little, it could be converted also into the head of a pantomime horse or the ass's head for Bottom in 'A Midsummer Night's Dream'. The Dragon's Head is similar, but more complicated and a little more difficult to make because of the concave curve in the front of the head.

Heads and large masks of this kind can be greatly strengthened and given a skin texture, readily apparent in the photograph of Tyrannosaurus Rex, by painting first with a standard household emulsion and then with one or more coats of a cement wash mixed to a fairly thick consistency. Emulsion paint can be applied inside and outside the mask, but preferably not both together, as this may make the paper very limp, thus causing distortion whilst drying. Before starting to paint a head or mask it is helpful to make a cylinder of card or something similar, to fit inside and hold it upright, as in the photographs.

For painting the features of masks, Rowney's p.v.a. colours, available in Britain in two sizes of plastic tubes, have proved excellent; they can be mixed with ordinary emulsion paint to provide additional tones. The colours are permanent and, when dry, they have a matt, washable surface which will withstand a good deal of wear and tear, almost inevitable in theatrical use. Poster or gouache paints are not recommended for this purpose, as they tend to transfer onto damp fingers and to rub off onto clothing. Do not forget to paint the inside of open mouths, where it can be seen; it adds greatly to the realism.

The Human Mask design provided here is, as the photograph shows, intended to cover the upper part of the head only, leaving the mouth and chin uncovered. This has the advantage that the actor's mouth and voice are not muffled by the mask; also the rigidity and, hence, the lifelessness, of a complete mask is avoided. The hair can be provided by a wig, fitted over the mask, or, as in the photograph, can be formed of pieces of paper, cut into narrow strips. Masks based upon this design, which can be altered considerably to suit many roles, are particularly suitable for fantasy characters such as Beanstalk Giants, Demon Kings, Wicked Witches and the like. Minor facial contours can be added and overlap joints can be covered with plaster or fibreglass filler paste.

One final point, which the professional may find most useful, is that heads and masks formed of paper provide an excellent base upon which to build a permanent surface of resin-bonded glass fibre. The paper masks can be constructed very quickly, with a little practice, so there is no need for heavy and expensive moulds. The sometimes tricky and lengthy business of removing a moulding from its mould is also avoided.

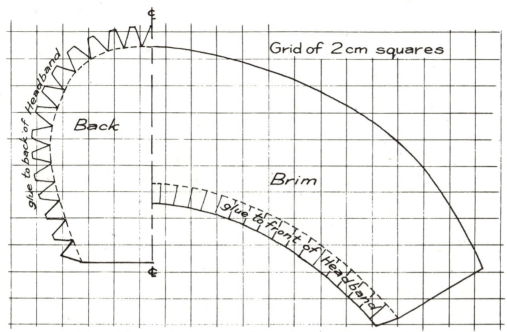

Grid of 2 cm squares

Back

Brim

glue to back of Headband

glue to front of Headband

The Headband is a rectangle 430 mm × 120 mm.

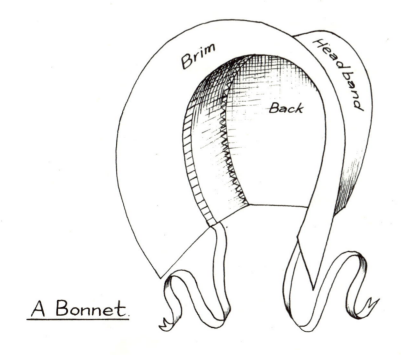

Brim

Headband

Back

A Bonnet.

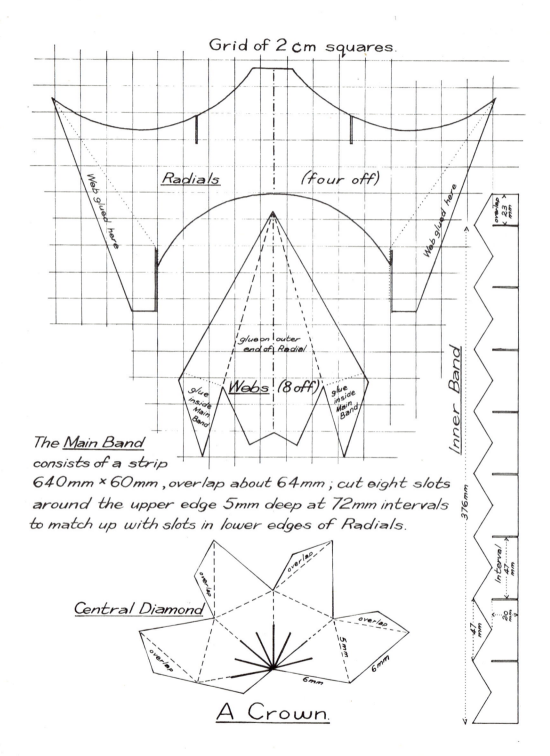

Grid of 2 cm squares.

Radials (four off)

Web glued here

Web glued here

glue on outer
end of Radial

Webs (8 off)

glue
inside
Main
Band

glue
inside
Main
Band

The *Main Band*
consists of a strip
640mm × 60mm , overlap about 64mm ; cut eight slots
around the upper edge 5mm deep at 72mm intervals
to match up with slots in lower edges of Radials.

Central Diamond

overlap

overlap

overlap

overlap

5mm

6mm

6mm

A Crown.

Inner Band

overlap 23 mm

376mm

Interval 47 mm

47 mm

20 mm

78

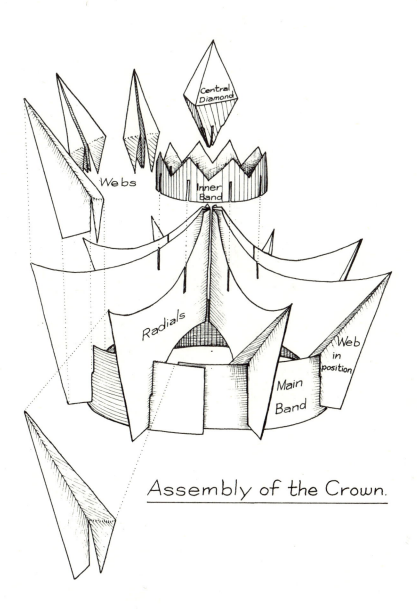

Central Diamond

Webs

Inner Band

Radials

Web in position

Main Band

Assembly of the Crown.

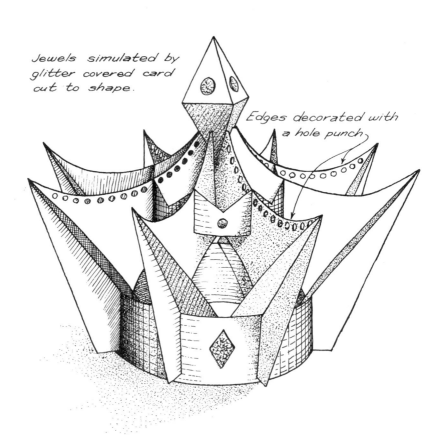

Jewels simulated by
glitter covered card
cut to shape.

Edges decorated with
a hole punch

The Completed Crown.

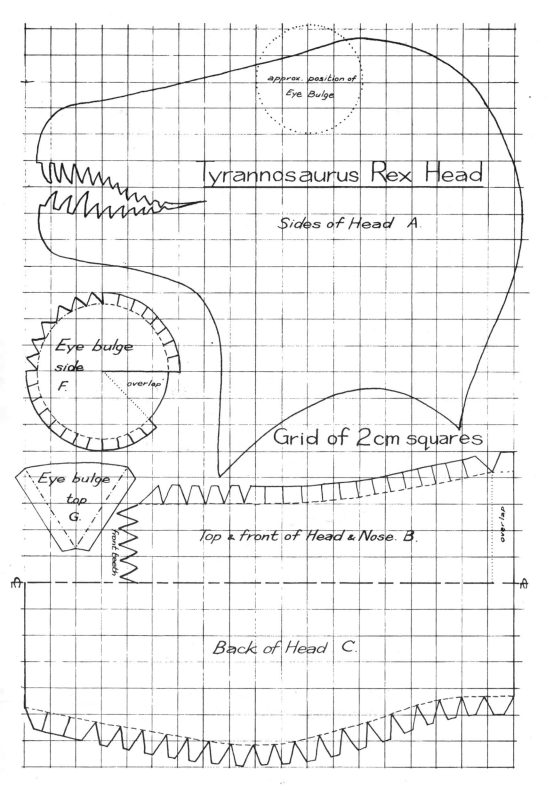

Tyrannosaurus Rex Head

Sides of Head A.

approx. position of
Eye Bulge

Eye bulge
side
F.

overlap

Eye bulge
top
G.

front teeth

Grid of 2cm squares

Top & front of Head & Nose. B.

overlap

Back of Head C.

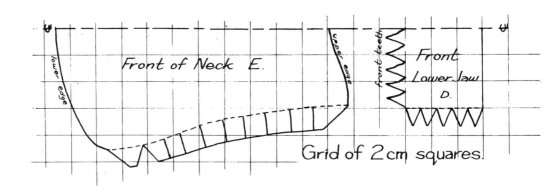

Front of Neck E.

lower edge

upper edge

front teeth

Front Lower Jaw D.

Grid of 2 cm squares.

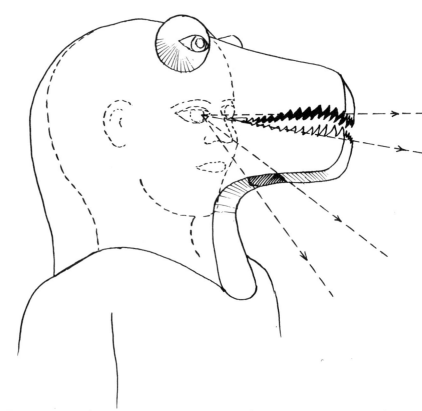

Note that the wearer has a clear view ahead,
both level and downwards.

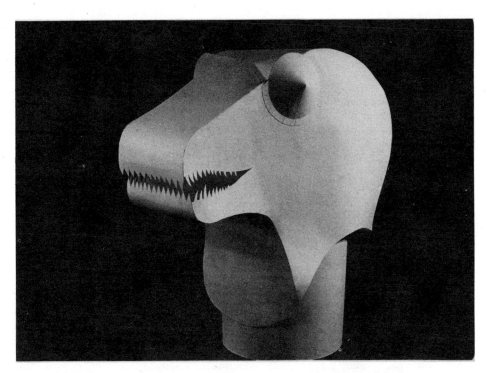

Unpainted Tyrannosaurus Rex Mask, made in 200 gsm cartridge paper.

Tyrannosaurus Rex Mask, made from 4-sheet card, painted with emulsion undercoat, textured with Snowcem and finished with p.v.a. paint.

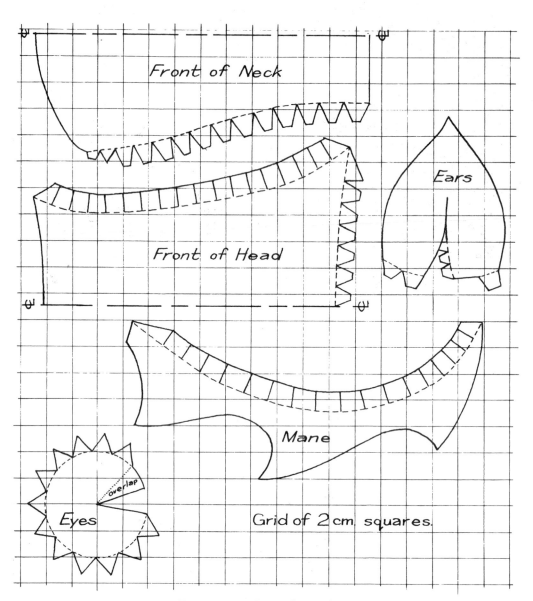

Front of Neck

Front of Head

Ears

Mane

over-lap

Eyes

Grid of 2 cm. squares.

Dragon's Head.

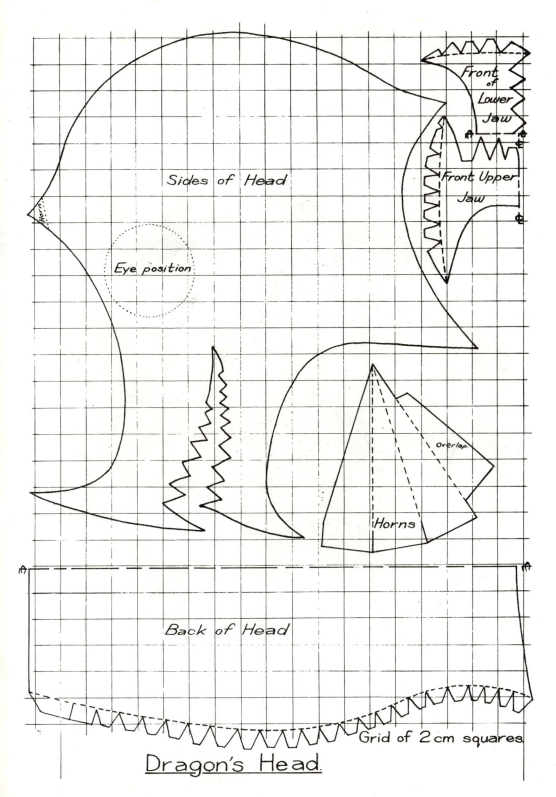

Sides of Head

Horn

Eye position

Front of Lower Jaw

Front Upper Jaw

Overlap.

Horns

Back of Head

Grid of 2 cm squares.

Dragon's Head.

Dragon's Head Mask, made from 4-sheet card, with emulsion undercoat, Snowcem texturing and finished with p.v.a. paint.

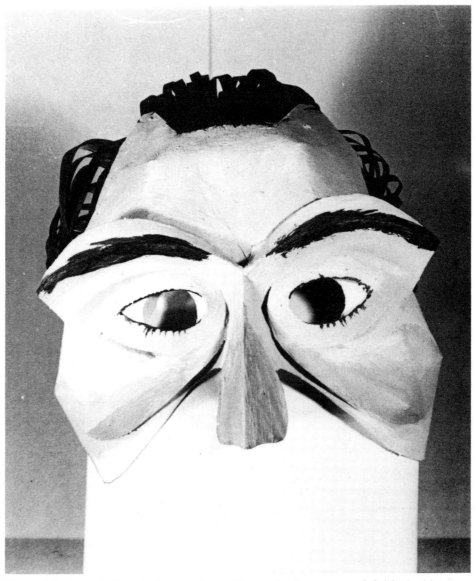

Human Mask, made from 4-sheet card, emulsion under Snowcem, and finished with p.v.a. paint.

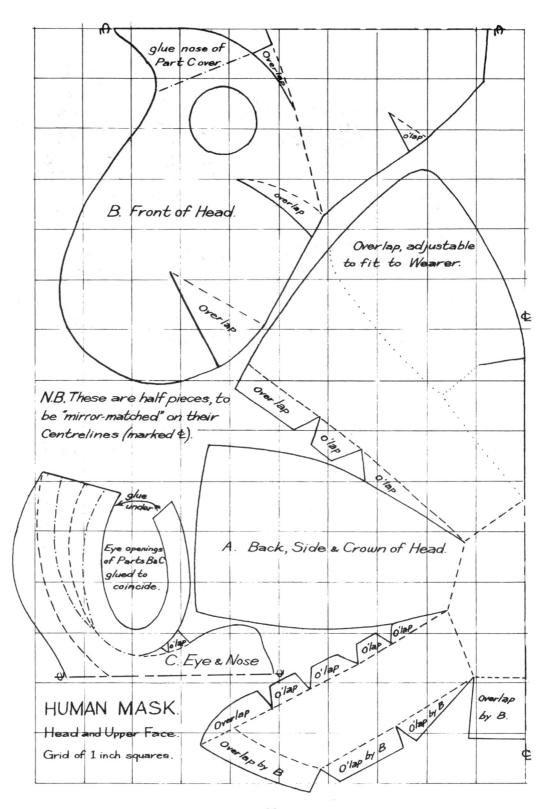

glue nose of Part C over.

Overlap

o'lap

overlap

Overlap, adjustable to fit to Wearer.

B. Front of Head.

Overlap

N.B. These are half pieces, to be "mirror-matched" on their Centrelines (marked ₵).

Overlap

o'lap

o'lap

glue under

Eye openings of Parts B & C glued to coincide.

A. Back, Side & Crown of Head.

o'lap

o'lap

o'lap

C. Eye & Nose

o'lap

o'lap

o'lap by B

Overlap

Overlap by B

o'lap by B

Overlap by B.

HUMAN MASK.
Head and Upper Face.
Grid of 1 inch squares.

8 Toys and Games

The necessity for care in selecting suitable material from which to make toys has been mentioned already in Chapter 5, but it cannot be overstressed, particularly if the toy is to be handled by small children. In this connection it must be pointed out immediately that the wire needed to make the toy WINDMILL is a potential hazard to very young children. Nevertheless this is a traditional toy of long standing, which uses a simple curled paper technique and therefore deserves inclusion in this book. All of the other items in this chapter are original in design, if not in use.

The DUMBELL constructional toy is more appreciated by girls than boys, as it provides scope for producing simple forms of jewellery, pendants, bangles, belts and the like. This toy, as well as the INTERLOCKING PANELS, is most attractive in a variety of bright colours. Both designs would lend themselves to mass production by stamping from plastic sheet, but they are not difficult to produce by hand. The Interlocking Panels can be scaled up to make quite large constructions, such as playhouses, by using hardboard instead of paper, but remember to allow additional clearance for the extra thickness of the material.

The INTERLOCKING LOGS are a new variant of a very old theme, but they can provide a basis for numerous toy structures, from farm fencing to cavalry fort. Again, this design can be scaled up to make larger units if required.

Puppets are always fascinating to children, and particularly glove puppets, for which a body is easily produced, but heads can be a stumbling block. The PUPPET'S HEAD (pages 97 and 98) is very straightforward to construct and is about the right size for a glove puppet. His expression can be altered quite easily, by turning the mouth so that the corners point down instead of up and by adjusting the cheek pieces slightly. There is a great deal of potential fun in painting the face as well, and, by changing the hair, a lady puppet's head is rapidly forthcoming. The same head could be used, of course, for a marionette or a doll. Only the left eye, ear and cheek have been drawn, but these are easily converted for the right side by transposing the pecked lines for pecked and dotted ones and vice versa.

The CHESS PIECES (pages 99–102) are also very simple in both design and construction, being basically cones fitted with identifying shapes on top. Simplicity is important here, because of the amount of handling to be anticipated, which would be likely to damage any fine detail work in paper. These pieces have proved to be quite strong enough for the purpose, made from 200 gsm cartridge paper and sprayed with glossy black and silver lacquer.

The CHESS BOARD (page 103) offers a slightly different challenge in that, although not being constantly handled, its surface must withstand constant

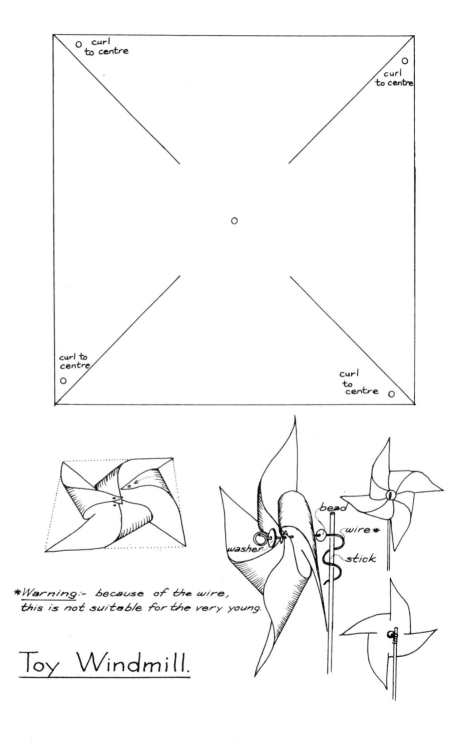

o curl
to centre

curl
to centre

curl to
centre

curl
to
centre

bead

wire *

washer

stick

*Warning:- because of the wire,
this is not suitable for the very young.

Toy Windmill.

abrasion by the pieces being moved. This can be overcome by applying a transparent, self-adhesive film over the whole playing area. Alternatively, contrasting coloured polyurethane lacquers could be used, or a polyurethane varnish over contrasting self-coloured papers.

DODECA-DICE (page 104) are so called because they are regular dodecahedra — having twelve identical faces. This idea is original to the author, but, being another variation on a very old theme, it may well have arisen elsewhere too. Such dice offer many possibilities not only in conjunction with the ubiquitous board games, such as 'Ludo' or 'Snakes and Ladders', where one will replace a pair of ordinary dice, but also in providing original and educational games by themselves. A great asset is that they are convenient to carry around. Two ways of marking such dice are shown in the drawing and another is included in the following suggestions for games using Dodeca-Dice only:

1. Mental Arithmetic

This requires two dice, one numbered one to twelve in the normal way, the other marked on opposing faces with the following six arithmetical instructions:

Add $(+x)$ Divide by $(\div x)$

Subtract $(-x)$ Square (x^2)

Multiply $(\times x)$ Decimal $(0.x)$

If played by two people, one throws the numbered dice, the other throws the dice carrying the instruction. The numbered dice is thrown first, followed by an instruction, then a second number, and so on. Each time a number is thrown the players take alternate turns to call out the solution of the sum up to that point, until a mistake is made by one player, which allows his opponent to win the game. The instructions 'Decimal' or 'Square' refer to the preceding number and require an immediate answer, which, if correct, would be followed by a second instruction before the next number. The instruction 'Decimal' means 'divide by 10'.

Example a
Player A throws 4,
Player B throws 'Multiply $(\times x)$'
Player A throws 3 and calls 'twelve'
Player B throws 'Add $(+x)$'
Player A throws 2 and player B calls 'fourteen'
Player B throws 'Decimal $(0.x)$' and player A calls 'one point four'
Player B throws 'Multiply $(\times x)$'
Player A throws 12, B calls 'sixteen point eight'
Player B throws 'Square (x^2)' and player A resigns!

91

The "Dumbell" Constructional Toy.

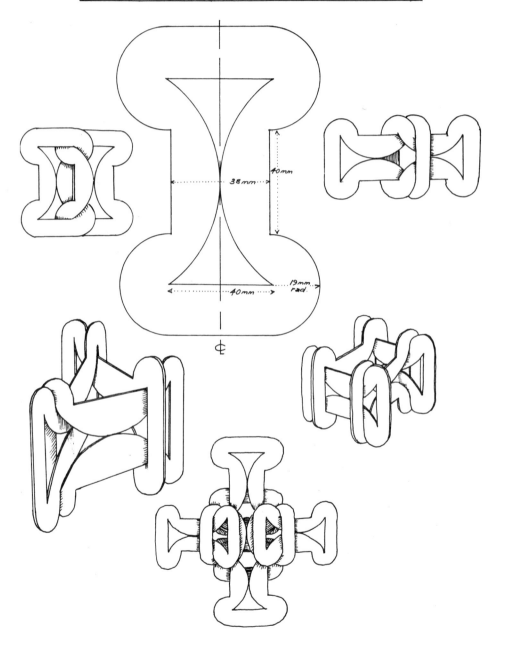

38mm

40mm

40mm

19mm
rad.

₵

Example b
Player A throws 6
Player B throws 'Square' and A calls 'thirty six'
Player B throws 'Subtract'
Player A throws 12 and B calls 'twenty four'
Player B throws 'Multiply'
Player A throws 11 and calls 'two hundred and forty four'
Player B challenges the answer and wins as the correct answer is 264.

To simplify the game, the instructions 'Square' and 'Decimal' may be omitted from the instruction dice and substituted by an extra one of the other four instructions. For a group game, one player is nominated as 'teacher' and throws the dice in sequence an agreed number of times to set a sum. The first of the remaining players to call out the correct answer wins and becomes 'teacher' for the next round.

2. Alphabet Soup

This game requires two dice marked with the alphabet as shown on the drawing. The players will require a pencil and paper each. Each player throws the dice, both together, until a vowel (A, E, I, O, or U) is one of the letters showing — Y may be counted as a vowel also, if the players so agree. The player then throws twice more and writes down the six letters that have appeared during his three throws. Each player's object then is to produce as many words as possible from the six letters he or she threw. One point is scored for every letter used in every word produced and the player with the highest score wins. A variation of this game for three or more players is for each player to throw in turn until each has thrown twice, the players noting *every* letter and then competing to produce the most words from the total of letters. The 'X or Z' and 'K or Q' options permit the use of either letter or both.

There are numerous other possible variations of marking the dice and games to play with them, but as this is a book about papercraft, this is not the place to describe all these possibilities and the reader may like to give his or her imagination full rein.

The 'POP UP' PICTURE (pages 105 and 106) is just a single example of a principle which can be varied, with all kinds of elaboration, to a virtually unlimited extent. Whole books of 'pop up' pictures used to be published for children, and some still are, although the amount of labour involved in the production results in a high price. This technique is particularly useful for making individual birthday cards for children, or for children to make for their relatives and friends. Its visual impact depends, to some extent, upon the choice of subject matter. Backgrounds of mountains, hills or imposing buildings are particularly effective, and, in the foreground, just one or two strong figures or objects of interest. An ability to draw well is not needed, for tracings from magazines, comics and newspapers can provide the required pictorial 'flats'. A good deal of fun can be generated by trying out different foreground figures against a selection of backgrounds, and deliberately preposterous situations can be devised purely for laughs. Colouring is quite important, but again there is no necessity for much artistic ability. Clear, bright, contrasting colours neatly used are all that is required for good effect.

The use of 'flats' to produce a three-dimensional scene is, of course, the everyday business of the theatre and the principles of 'pop up' pictures are easily extended to produce model theatres. A variety of scenery can be designed and made for such a theatre, using all the paper sculpture techniques, from the very simple to the most complex. This is in the Victorian tradition of toy theatre, for which sheets of printed scenery and actors, 'penny plain, twopence coloured', were published for children to cut out and use.

The ingenuity of some Victorian Christmas and birthday cards has to be studied to be fully appreciated. Not content with the simple 'pop up' picture, of the type illustrated here, the designers devised miniature masterpieces of paper sculpture, often incorporating fine threads as part of the mechanism, to make apparently solid structures arise magically from the centre of an innocent folded card. Among a collection recently examined by the author was a fully rigged model of *HMS Victory*, a tramcar with people in it, a large bouquet of flowers, and Cleopatra's elaborately decorated and crewed Nile barge.

Unfortunately the very complexity of these Victorian designs precludes a detailed description of them here; indeed, a separate book could be written about them. Examples are available for study in many museums, however, and the enthusiast can bear in mind that, although the components were usually printed, the cards were invariably assembled by hand, so the techniques of their makers can be re-learnt today. Furthermore, we have the advantages of greatly improved materials, particularly glues and paints, which will withstand constant flexing far better than the original materials did. Unfortunately it was the poor quality of the glues used that caused the eventual disintegration of most of these old cards. However, if you do find an example in otherwise good condition, it is a relatively simple matter to copy the unglued component parts and make a modern replica. Antiquarians might frown on the repair of an original with modern glue, but the point could be debated if it resulted in restoration to full working order.

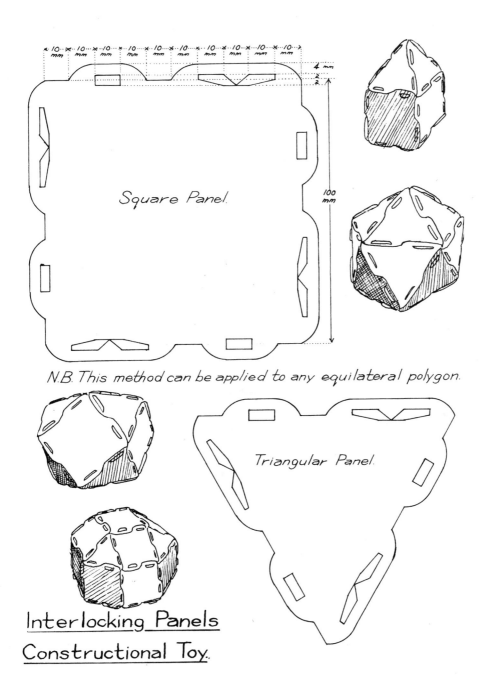

10 mm 10 mm 10 mm 10 mm 10 mm 10 mm 10 mm 10 mm 10 mm 10 mm

4 mm
2 mm
2

Square Panel.

100 mm

N.B. This method can be applied to any equilateral polygon.

Triangular Panel.

Interlocking Panels
Constructional Toy.

Interlocking End Pieces.

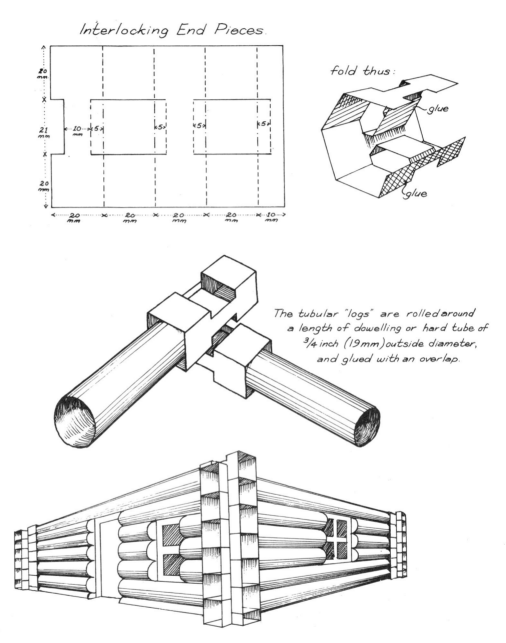

fold thus :

glue

glue

The tubular "logs" are rolled around a length of dowelling or hard tube of ¾ inch (19mm) outside diameter, and glued with an overlap.

<u>Interlocking Logs : Constructional Toy.</u>

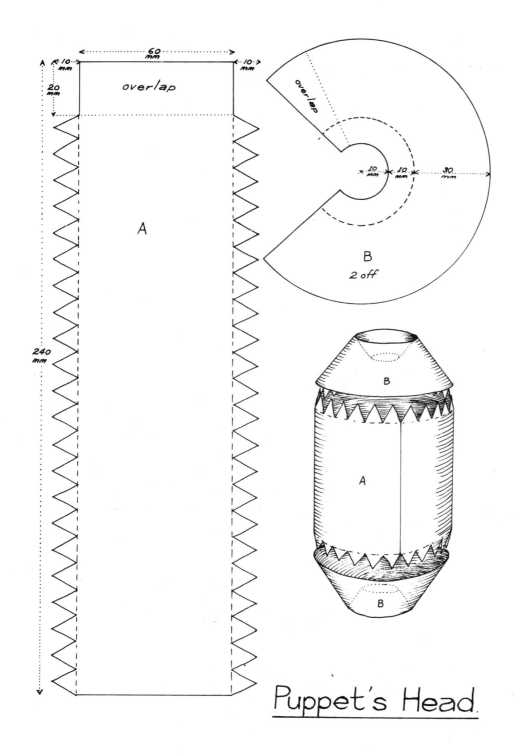

60
mm

10
mm

10
mm

20
mm

overlap

A

240
mm

overlap

10
mm

10
mm

30
mm

B

2 off

B

A

B

Puppet's Head.

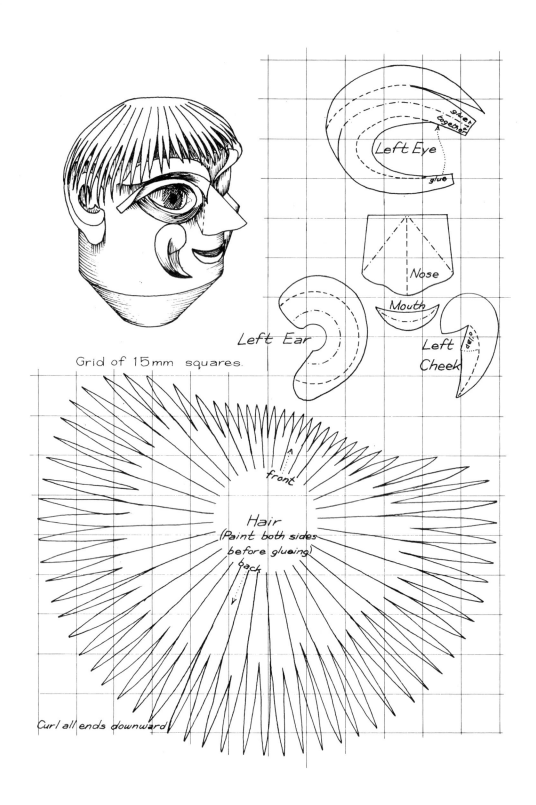

Left Eye

glue together

glue

Nose

Mouth

Left Ear

Left Cheek

glue

Grid of 15 mm squares.

front

Hair
(Paint both sides
before glueing)
back

Curl all ends downward

The Kings and Queens are based on cones formed from the four quadrants of a circle, radius 85 mm. All other pieces are similarly based on cones made from quadrants of 80mm radius circles, the overlap in the larger cones being 15mm and in the smaller ones 12mm at the base of the cone. Construction is easier if the top 20mm (centre circle 20mm rad.) is removed first.

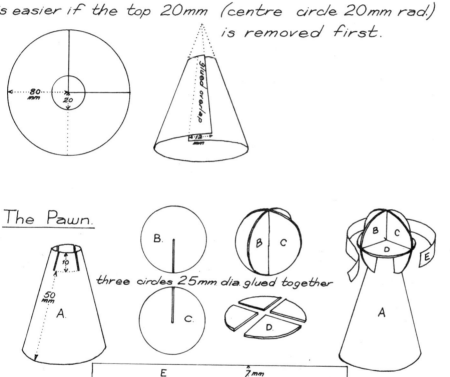

The Pawn.

three circles 25mm dia. glued together

strip E is glued around the horizontal circumference of D.

A Chess Set

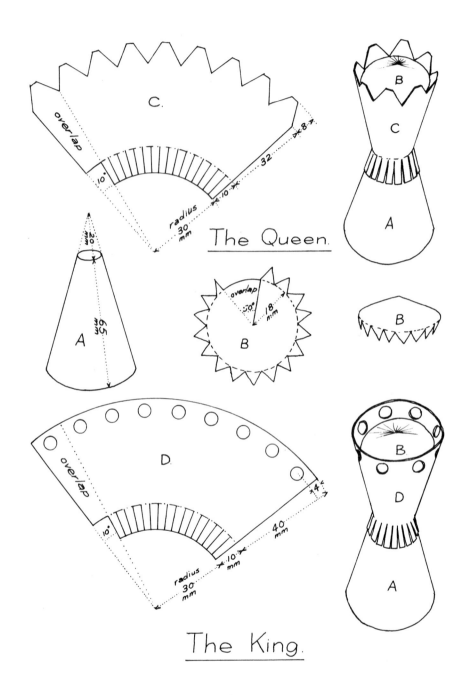

C.

overlap

10°

32

radius
30
mm

8

10

The Queen.

B

C

A

A

65
mm

20°

overlap

30°

18
mm

B

B

D

overlap

10°

40
mm

radius
30
mm

10
mm

4

B

D

A

The King.

100

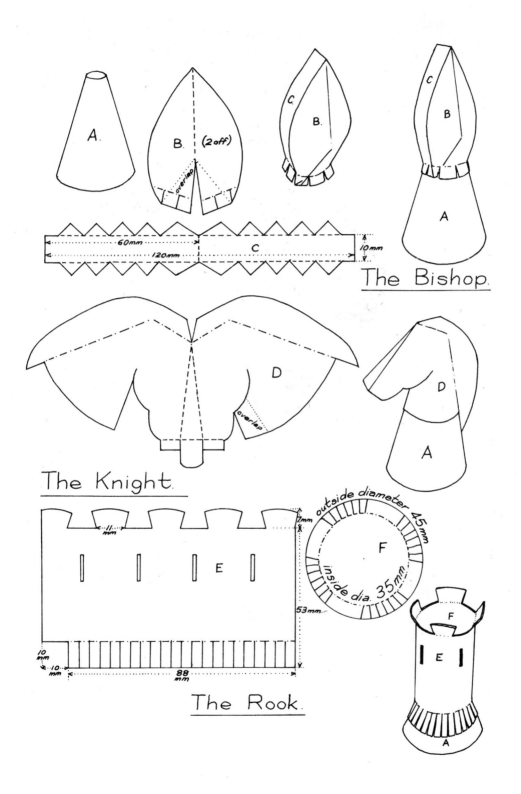

A.

B. (2 off)

overlap

C.

B.

C

B.

C

B.

A

The Bishop.

60mm

120mm

10mm

D

overlap

D

A

The Knight.

7mm

11 mm

E

53mm

10 mm

10mm

88 mm

The Rook.

outside diameter 45mm

F

inside dia. 35mm

F

E

A

Chess Pieces, made from 200 gsm cartridge paper, sprayed with silver lacquer.

Chess Set. The men are made from 200 gsm cartridge paper, sprayed with silver and black gloss lacquer. The board is made from 4-sheet card, sprayed with silver and copper colour lacquer, glued to a mounting board and framed by triangular box section. The frame is covered in wood grain patterned self-adhesive film and the board is covered in transparent self-adhesive plastic film.

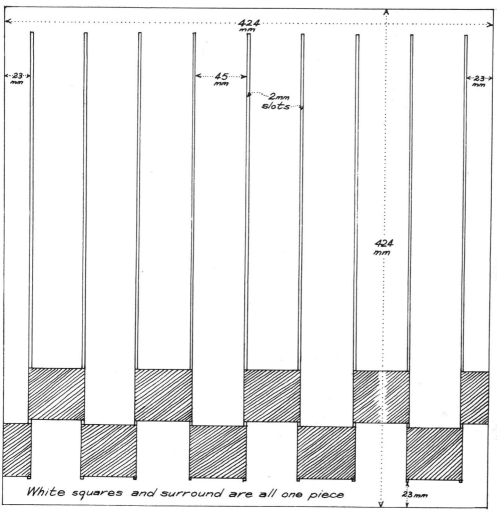

424
mm

23 mm

45 mm

2mm slots

424 mm

White squares and surround are all one piece

23 mm

428 mm

Black squares are formed by interweaving eight black strips alternately between the white strips, through the slots provided, and then glueing the ends in position. The whole assembly may be mounted on stiff board and framed.

Chess or Draughts Board.

On a numbered
dodecahedral (12 faced)
dice, the figures on
opposing faces add
up to make 13,
therefore :-

12 opposes 1
11   "   2
10   "   3
9   "   4
8   "   5
7   "   6

A template made from a
tracing of this pentagon will
help you to draw the twelve
faces of the dice in
accordance with the
diagram and to a
convenient size.

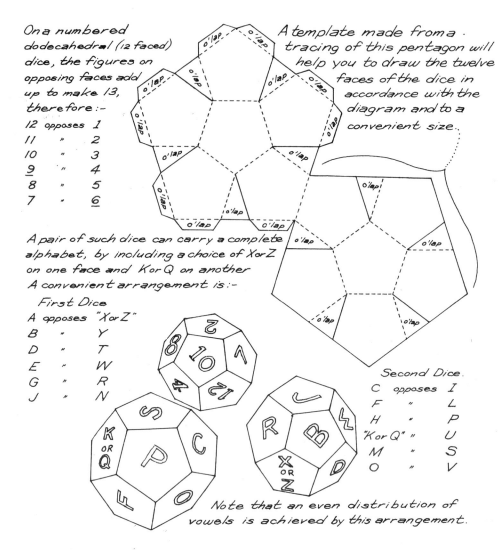

A pair of such dice can carry a complete
alphabet, by including a choice of X or Z
on one face and K or Q on another
A convenient arrangement is :-

First Dice

A opposes "X or Z"
B   "   Y
D   "   T
E   "   W
G   "   R
J   "   N

Second Dice.

C   opposes   I
F   "   L
H   "   P
"K or Q"   "   U
M   "   S
O   "   V

Note that an even distribution of
vowels is achieved by this arrangement.

One dice with twelve faces can replace two normal dice with
only six faces each. See text for suggested games.

Dodeca-dice.

Outlines to be cut are drawn in heavy lines

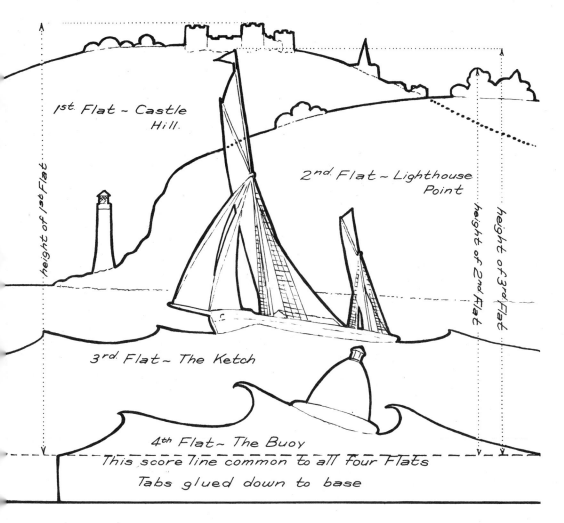

1st. Flat ~ Castle Hill.

height of 1st Flat

2nd. Flat ~ Lighthouse Point

height of 3rd Flat

height of 2nd Flat

3rd. Flat ~ The Ketch

4th Flat ~ The Buoy

This score line common to all four Flats

Tabs glued down to base

"Pop Up" Picture.

105

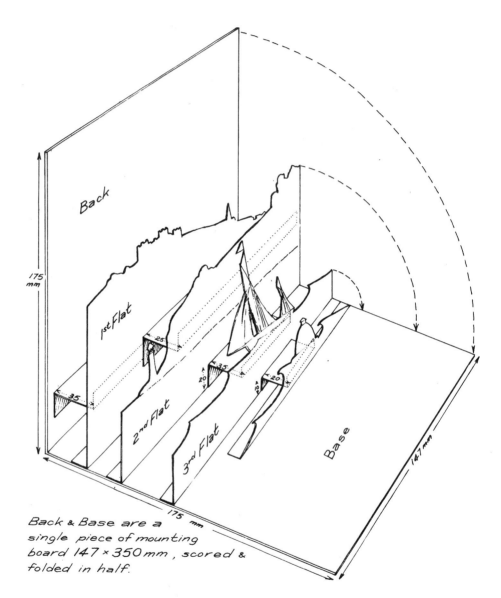

Back

175
mm

1st Flat

35

25

2nd Flat

20 35

3rd Flat

20 20

Base

147 mm

175 mm

Back & Base are a
single piece of mounting
board 147 × 350 mm, scored &
folded in half.

Schematic diagram of complete assembly

9 Items for the Home

Articles used around the home need to be able to stand up to handling and, if possible, they should be washable, so it would be better to make most of the items in this chapter in the plastic materials which are sold by handicraft shops for lampshade making. Many of these are well suited to treatment by paper-craft techniques; they can be scored and folded, and they can also be glued with the appropriate type of p.v.c. or plastic glue. Materials used for lampshades must be able to withstand prolonged heat without distortion or, more important, catching fire. There are two types of inexpensive material available in Britain which can be recommended for lampshades: 'Snolin' is white, and 'Acelon' is a resin-coated fabric produced in a range of pastel colours. Both are translucent and have a fabric finish. Used in conjunction with p.v.c. ribbon to bind around the rings, and a suitable p.v.c. glue, a wide variety of lampshade designs can be achieved.

These plastic sheet materials are normally supplied in rolls and they do not have the same finish on both sides. This can pose a minor problem, in that the material may have taken up a permanent curve from the roll, with the wrong side on the outside of the curve. This can be overcome quite simply, by ironing the recalcitrant piece of sheet with a warm iron — not hot, or it may distort or melt the material. It is sensible to lay a sheet of paper over the plastic before ironing.

All of the lampshade designs, including the Five Sided Lantern, are measured to fit over the present standard 6 in. (about 152 mm) diameter rings, but it is, of course, a relatively easy matter to scale the design dimensions up or down to suit larger or smaller rings for a particular purpose. The author's aim has been to provide workable examples primarily in order to stimulate the development of the reader's own ideas and the design possibilities for lampshades, even on a simple cylindrical base, are endless. For instance, all of the design variations shown for architrave 'mouldings' in Chapter 6 can be applied to columns of a Columnar Cylindrical Lampshade.

The simple construction technique for lampshades suggested here is to bind spirally one pendant and one plain ring, so as to cover the circumference completely, with the inexpensive $1\frac{1}{4}$ in. (32 mm) wide plastic ribbon, available, in various colours, from the same sources as the other lampshade materials. This ribbon can be secured easily with p.v.c. glue which tends to melt and therefore welds it. The cylindrical base is cut, and its overlap glued, so that the covered rings are a comfortable push-fit inside it. When the overlap is dry, the covered rings can be positioned inside, a thin band of p.v.c. glue being laid just above the upper one and just below the lower one. The rings are then eased gently onto their respective bands of glue and left to dry. The outer decoration, as it is completed, can be glued to the inner cylinder, with the advantage of the strength provided by the already mounted rings and the additional ease of handling they offer. The columns of the Columnar Cylindrical Lampshade do not need to be glued, as they are secured in place adequately by their hooks and by the spacers designed on the edges of the central cylinder.

THE FIVE SIDED LANTERN has a base designed to fit it, but it could be used as a hanging shade for a porch light, for instance, by omitting the base and placing a 6 in. (152 mm) pendant ring inside. If mains electricity is to be used, it is essential that all the materials must be non-inflammable. Remember that the 'roof' of the lantern will certainly be heated to some extent by the lamp below it, so use a low wattage bulb, at least until you have made sure, by testing, that a higher wattage is perfectly safe. The lantern can be made to this design, or with variations to taste, in light aluminium sheet, cut with snips and secured with pop rivets instead of glue. For theatrical or carnival use these lanterns are ideal and can be made safely in paper or card if the lamp inside is just a torch bulb powered by small dry batteries. These lanterns, containing such small, dry battery-powered lamps, are particularly recommended for carol singing parties at Christmas time.

THE FOUR STRAND PLAITED BOOKMARK (page 114) is included here because it is a useful way of using up offcuts of lampshade material. One is not limited to four strands, of course; any number of strands from three upwards can be plaited in this way. Note that it is easier to start from the centre, securing the strands with a little glue, and working outwards towards the ends, rather than from one end to the other.

THE WOVEN PAPER CYLINDRICAL CONTAINER (page 115), made to the dimensions indicated, would be suitable for a gift of home-made sweets or biscuits. It could be scaled up to make a waste-paper basket or plant pot cover. Containers made in this way are remarkably strong and flexible. It is worth mentioning here that lampshade designs are also applicable to containers of this kind, and that this woven paper technique could be used equally well to produce lampshades, table napkin rings, bangles and a variety of decorative coverings. The basic 'over one, under one' weave can be varied by going 'over one, under two' or vice versa and so on; colours also can be intermingled in various ways.

THE BOOK-END, as illustrated on pages 116–118, was made in 200 gsm cartridge paper and sprayed with p.v.c. upholstery paint, to provide a hard wearing surface. It was designed for use with paperback books and the weight of the books themselves, bearing down on the base of the book-end, provides all the weight necessary to prevent shift sideways. The design of the book-end contains great vertical rigidity, so that, if linked together by a cross-member at the back, two of these book-ends would form a satisfactory book rack. The one provision they do require is adequate horizontal support beneath, such as a window sill or mantelshelf.

1.

Cover a pendant and a plain ring by binding with plastic ribbon. Secure ends with p.v.c. glue.

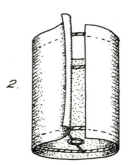

2.

Glue bound rings about 20mm. inside edges of lining tube.

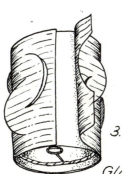

3.

4.

Glue facing material, with pre-cut design, around outside the lining.

Many design variations can be based upon a cylindrical liner.

Cylindrical Base Lampshades.

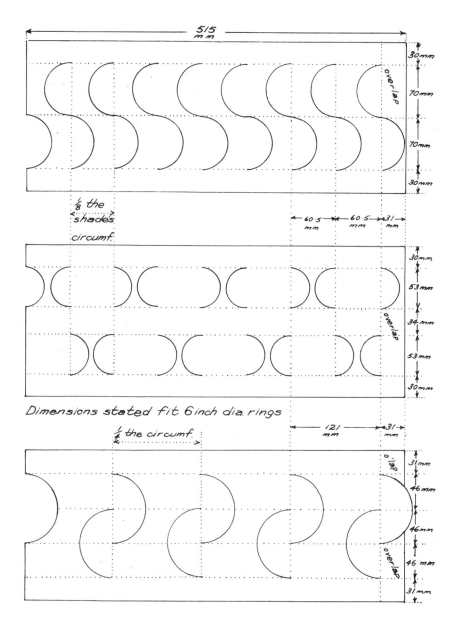

Cylindrical Lampshades. Cut circle designs.

Line inside with a plain cylinder of a contrasting colour.
Use non-inflammable materials for lampshades.

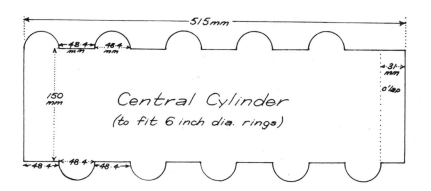

515mm

48·4 mm   48·4 mm

Central Cylinder

(to fit 6 inch dia. rings)

150 mm

·31· mm

o'lap

48·4   48·4   48·4

Outer Columns ~ ten required

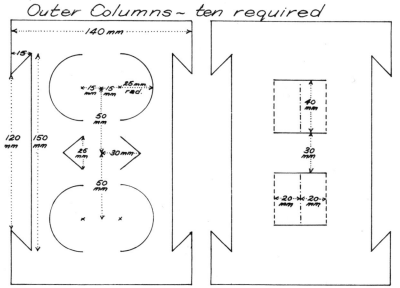

140 mm

·15·

·15· mm   ·15· mm   25mm rad.

50 mm

120 mm   150 mm

·25· mm   ·30mm·

50 mm

40 mm

30 mm

·20· mm   ·20· mm

Columnar Cylindrical Lampshades.

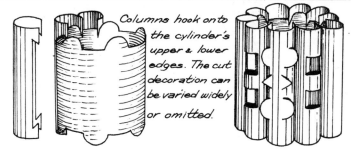

Columns hook onto
the cylinder's
upper & lower
edges. The cut
decoration can
be varied widely
or omitted.

Five-Sided Lantern.

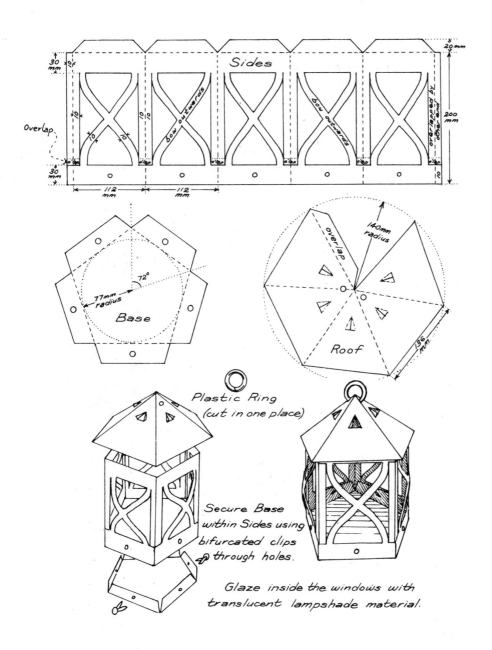

Sides

30 mm

20 mm

200 mm

overlap.

30 mm

112 mm   112 mm

bow outwards

bow outwards

overlapped by the end

Base

72°

77mm radius

Roof

140mm radius

overlap

136 mm

Plastic Ring
(cut in one place)

Secure Base
within Sides using
bifurcated clips
through holes.

Glaze inside the windows with
translucent lampshade material.

A Five Sided Lantern.

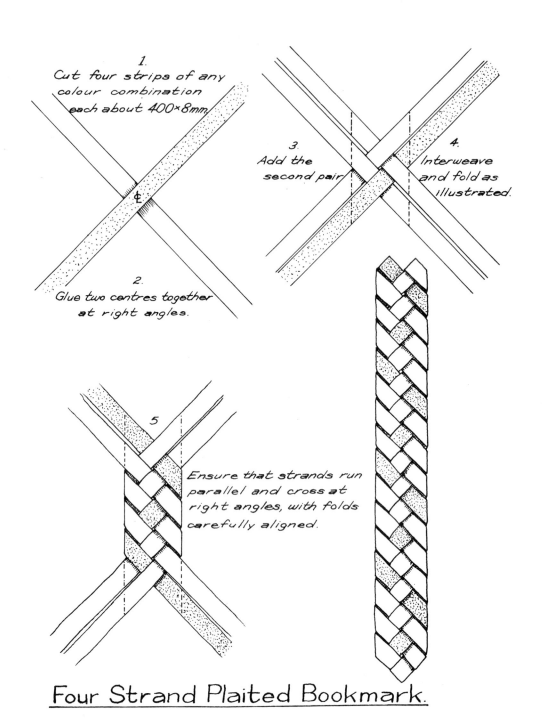

1.
Cut four strips of any colour combination each about 400×8mm.

2.
Glue two centres together at right angles.

3.
Add the second pair.

4.
Interweave and fold as illustrated.

5.
Ensure that strands run parallel and cross at right angles, with folds carefully aligned.

Four Strand Plaited Bookmark.

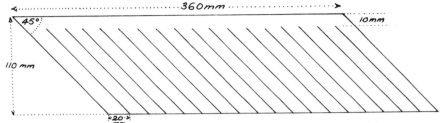

360mm

45°

110 mm

20 mm

10mm

1. Cut two pieces like this.

2. Overlap & glue the end strips of each, forming two cylinders.

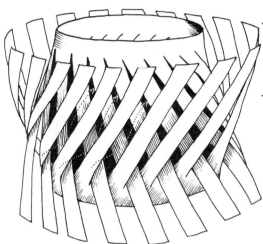

3. "Marry" the two cylinders as illustrated, with strips alternating upward and downward.

4. Interweave the strips in both directions to top and bottom.

5. Glue ends of strips inside.

6. Cut disc with tabs to form bottom and glue tabs inside the base.

Woven Paper Cylindrical Container.

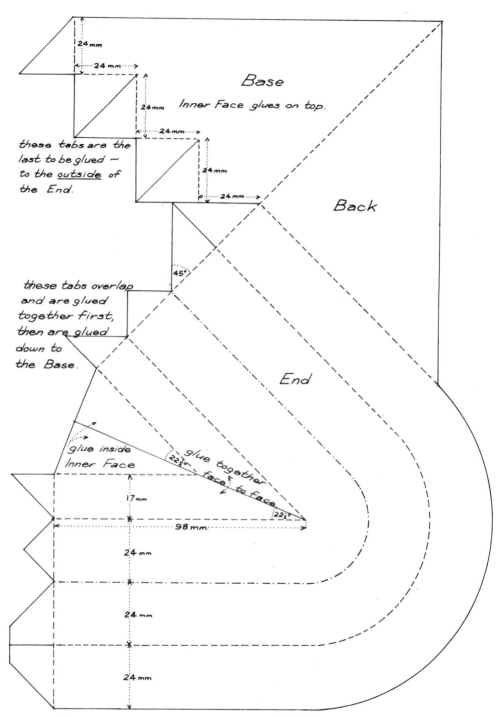

24 mm

24 mm

24 mm

24 mm

24 mm

24 mm

Base

Inner Face glues on top.

these tabs are the last to be glued — to the <u>outside</u> of the End.

Back

45°

these tabs overlap and are glued together first, then are glued down to the Base.

End

glue inside Inner Face

glue together face to face

22½°

22½°

17 mm

98 mm

24 mm

24 mm

24 mm

Book-End : Outside and back.

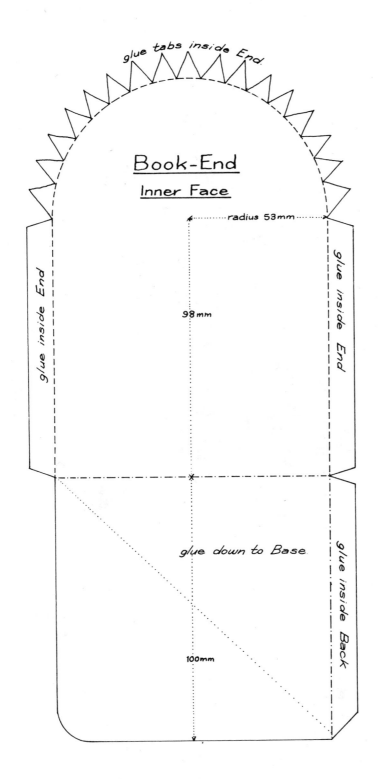

glue tabs inside End

Book-End
Inner Face

radius 53mm

98mm

glue inside End

glue inside End

glue down to Base

glue inside Back

100mm

Completed Book-End.

10 Decorations

Early in this book, in Chapter 3, some of the decorative possibilities of leaves
and foliage were mentioned and the projects included Tudor roses and a wheat-
sheaf. I have used large paper leaves a metre or more in length, sprayed with
red, yellow and gold paint, to decorate the walls of a school hall for an autumn
dance, to great effect. However, these have been stylized representations rather
than attempts to imitate the real. From an aesthetic point of view, it would be
probably the general opinion that imitating nature is not to be recommended.
Nevertheless, artificial flowers continue to be popular, whether they closely
represent nature or not, and the crêpe paper carnations and roses described in
this chapter do resemble their natural models quite closely. The carnations, in
particular, are so accurate a representation that they are commonly taken for
real, even at close quarters.

Whether one approves of artificial flowers or not, they are often desirable
for stage use. The technique described in this chapter for making artificial roses
from crêpe paper was invented by the author in response to a request for a large
quantity of red roses for a production of 'Oliver' by Tarporley High School in
Cheshire, England. The song 'Will you buy my sweet red roses?' has to be
accompanied by a credible offer of the flowers themselves, or it becomes farcical.
Similarly, stage wreaths and bouquets of more than merely acceptable appearance
can be made from crêpe paper flowers with all the advantages of semi-permanence
and low cost. Gift ribbon flowers and birds are also well suited for stage use as
hat trimmings, where their bright colours and stylized form can be used to good
effect.

It can be said in criticism here, and with some justification, that gift ribbon
is not paper. Nevertheless, it can respond well to some, although not all, paper
sculpture techniques. Also anything that can be done with gift ribbon can be
done with paper, with the addition of a little glue. The GIFT RIBBON FLOWERS
can be made just as well with other materials. For instance, the offcuts of
'Acelon' from lampshades make most attractive, non-representational flowers,
using this method and if a small arrangement is made up, with a tiny lamp
hidden inside each flower, they can be quite beautiful as a decorative centrepiece.

Unfortunately, the broader widths of gift ribbon are becoming difficult to
find in the shops, so the size of flowers made with such ribbon is severely
restricted. They are an attractive decoration on gift parcels and have been used
successfully to make small boutonnières for ladies at a special dance. As
table decorations for a party and to add colour to a Christmas wreath of holly
and ivy these bright little flowers can be used to particularly good effect.

The GIFT RIBBON BIRDS are similarly restricted in size by the width of the available material, but their design is freely adaptable and can be effective in other materials, such as metal foil and fabric ribbons as well as paper. A wise choice of colours and care in producing the feathery appearance are of particular importance. These birds make very attractive decorations for gift parcels, but are also suitable for mobiles and they are, of course, particularly at home adding colour to a Christmas tree.

The CREPE PAPER CARNATIONS are the most realistic paper flowers that can be made quickly and without attempting to copy natural construction. This method of making them was demonstrated to me by my wife's hairdresser, to whom it had been taught by a flower arranging enthusiast, but its real origin is not known. I have simplified the method slightly, without affecting the realism of the finished product. I found also that, by brushing the tips of a finished flower's petals with a broad felt tipped pen of a suitable colour, the authentic variegated tints of real carnations can be accurately simulated. This looks most effective if you apply red to the tips of the petals of white crêpe paper carnations.

The procedure illustrated for making CREPE PAPER TULIP AND ROSE is original. The rose is developed via a tulip shape, but the texture of crêpe paper is really more suited to the rose than to the tulip, which in nature has a waxy gloss. When cutting the petal shapes in the basic strip (see the top diagram on the first page illustrating the Tulip and Rose), it is advisable to avoid cutting all the petals of the same width, otherwise when the strip is rolled up, the petals may lie neatly one above the other in rows, which does not happen in nature. Vary the width of the petals between about 25 mm and 50 mm, so that their divisions are staggered around the flower and are overlapped by the next row of petals.

When buying crêpe paper for flowers it is well worth choosing the best quality, for the little extra it may cost will be repaid amply by the better results and easier working. Poor quality crêpe paper tears easily in stretching and tends to lose its colour and become transparent when stretched. It is also advisable to to choose colours which are normally found in nature — plain reds, pinks, yellows and whites for roses; for carnations avoid yellow, but add mauve. Do not be tempted into emulating the more exotic colours of the nurseryman's catalogue; they are hard enough to believe at a flower show and in paper they look truly artificial.

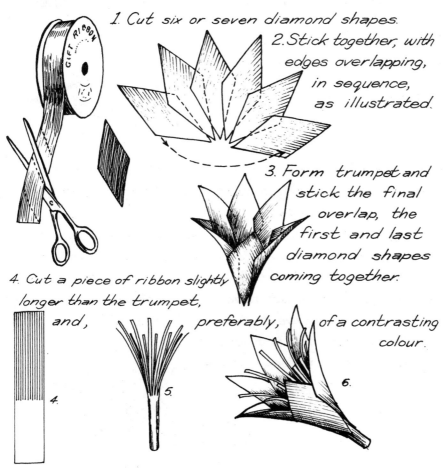

1. Cut six or seven diamond shapes.

2. Stick together, with edges overlapping, in sequence, as illustrated.

3. Form trumpet and stick the final overlap, the first and last diamond shapes coming together.

4. Cut a piece of ribbon slightly longer than the trumpet, and, preferably, of a contrasting colour.

Cut about ½ the length into narrow strips.

5. Roll across the width and glue, to form a thin tube at one end, with strips splayed out at the other.

6. Apply a little glue to the tubular end and push it down inside the trumpet.

Gift Ribbon Flowers.

Alternative "Narcissus" Type of Centre.

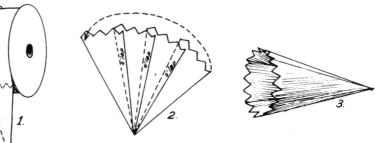

1. Cut two pieces of ribbon about 4cms. long,
using pinking shears. Cut each piece into
two diagonally, using straight scissors.
2. Stick the four pieces together, edges
overlapping and points together fan shaped.
3. Form into pointed trumpet by overlapping and
sticking the first and last edges.
4. Apply a little glue to the point of
the small trumpet and push
it down inside the outer one.

——— " ———

Green tie-wire stem.
Green ribbon leaves.

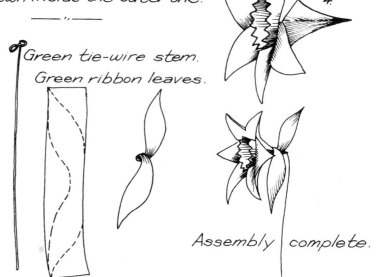

Assembly complete.

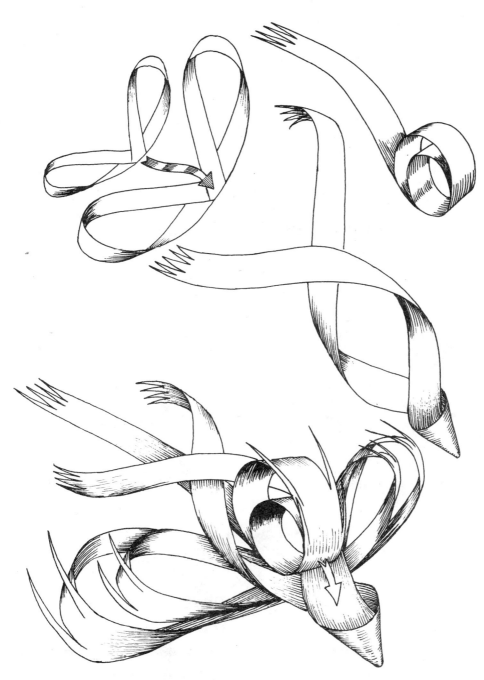

Gift Ribbon Bird.

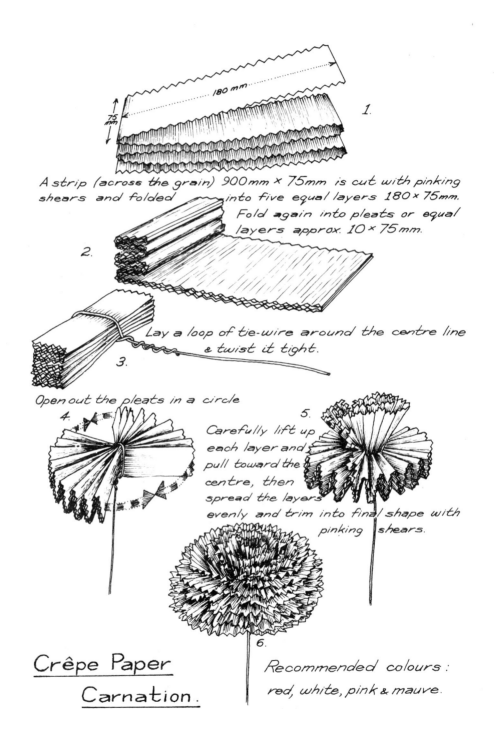

1.

A strip (across the grain) 900mm × 75mm is cut with pinking shears and folded into five equal layers 180 × 75mm.

Fold again into pleats or equal layers approx. 10 × 75 mm.

2.

Lay a loop of tie-wire around the centre line & twist it tight.

3.

Open out the pleats in a circle

4.

5.

Carefully lift up each layer and pull toward the centre, then spread the layers evenly and trim into final shape with pinking shears.

6.

Crêpe Paper
Carnation.

Recommended colours: red, white, pink & mauve.

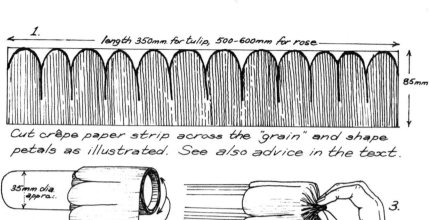

1.

length 350mm for tulip, 500-600mm for rose

85mm

Cut crêpe paper strip across the "grain" and shape petals as illustrated. See also advice in the text.

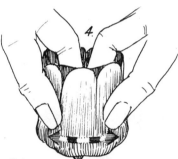

35mm dia. approx.

2.
Roll around tube or rod,

apply glue

3.

Pull ⅓ over tube end and pinch the base closed.

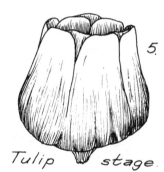

4.

Stretch to widen base.

5.

Tulip stage.

6.

Turn over and stretch inside the upper edges of the outer petals.

Note: It is important to choose colours that occur naturally in a flower.

Crêpe Paper
Tulip and Rose.

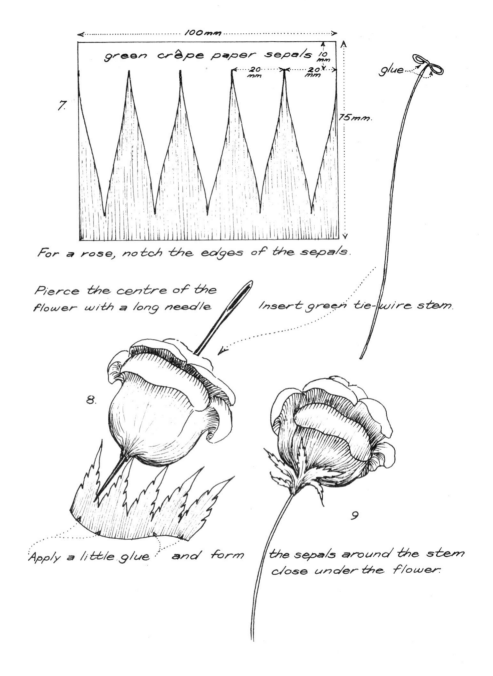

100mm

green crêpe paper sepals

10 mm

20 mm   20 mm

75mm.

glue

7.

For a rose, notch the edges of the sepals.

Pierce the centre of the
flower with a long needle

Insert green tie-wire stem.

8.

9

Apply a little glue   and form   the sepals around the stem
close under the flower.

Conclusion

In conclusion the reader is again urged to fully use his or her imagination and to try out new ideas in paper. Too many good ideas are never put to a practical test because of the originator's diffidence, so be willing to 'have a go'. The world can always use a good idea and, if it can be proved in paper, it could hardly be cheaper, even if the finished product is intended to be gold plated. Constantly bear in mind that what can be made in paper can be made also in many other materials. This is particularly true of plastic sheet, of which there are already many kinds and no doubt many more will be developed as time passes.

Utilisation of leisure time is a problem for many, however strange that may sound to some, and it seems likely to be a problem that will loom ever larger in the industrialised world during the next decade or two. Paper being a familiar, clean, inexpensive and widely available material, provides a hobbyist's construction medium which should be of general appeal, yet it is still overlooked or ignored because those who might use it are not aware of its full potential. Hopefully this book will help to increase that awareness.

Index